THE LATIN DELI

THE

Judith Ortiz Cofer

LATiN

Prose and Poetry

DELI

The University of Georgia Press
Athens and London

© 1993 by Judith Ortiz Cofer
All rights reserved
Published by the University of Georgia Press
Athens, Georgia 30602

Designed by Sandra Strother Hudson
Set in 10.5 on 14 Electra by Tseng Information Systems, Inc.
Printed and bound by Maple-Vail
The paper in this book meets the guidelines
for permanence and durability of the Committee on
Production Guidelines for Book Longevity
of the Council on Library Resources.

Printed in the United States of America
97 96 95 94 93 C 5 4 3 2 1

Library of Congress Cataloging in Publication Data

Ortiz Cofer, Judith, 1952–
The Latin deli : prose and poetry / Judith Ortiz Cofer.
p.   cm.
ISBN 0-8203-1556-7 (alk. paper)
1. Puerto Rican women—United States—Literary collections.
2. Women—Puerto Rico—Literary collections.   I. Title.
PS3565.R7737L37   1993
810.8'0352042—dc20   92-44782

British Library Cataloging in Publication Data available

TO MY DAUGHTER, TANYA

I know who I am, and who I may be if I choose.

—Don Quixote

Contents

Acknowledgments

Grateful acknowledgment is made to the following magazines in which some of the works in this book first appeared, sometimes in slightly different versions or under different titles:

Americas Review: "Juana: An Old Story," "Paciencia," "Saint Rose of Lima," and "The Latin Deli: An Ars Poetica." Copyright Arte Publico Press of the University of Houston, 1988, 1991, and 1992. Reprinted with permission of the publisher.

Antioch Review: "The Life of an Echo"

Bilingual Review/La Revista Bilingüe (vol. 17, no. 2, p. 161): "My Grandfather's Hat." Copyright 1992, The Bilingual Review/Press of Arizona State University (Tempe, Ariz.). Reprinted by permission of the publisher.

Cream City Review: "Orar: To Pray"

Georgia Review: Nada

Glamour: "How to Get a Baby" and *The Myth of the Latin Woman: I Just Met A Girl Named Maria*

Hayden's Ferry Review: Five A.M.: Writing As Ritual

Indiana Review: "The Game"

Kenyon Review: "They Never Grew Old," "An Early Mystery," "A Legion of Dark Angels," *Not For Sale,* and *The Witch's Husband*

Lullwater Review: "Blood"

Missouri Review: Advanced Biology

National Forum: "The Lesson of the Teeth"

Nomad: "Absolution in the New Year"

Parnassus: "Nothing Wasted," "To Grandfather, Now Forgetting," and "Vida"

Passages North: "Fever" and "Counting"

Prairie Schooner: "Unspoken," "Hostages to Fortune," and "The Changeling." Reprinted from *Prairie Schooner* by permission of the University of Nebraska Press. Copyright 1992 University of Nebraska Press.

Sing Heavenly Muse! "Women Who Love Angels"

South Florida Poetry Review: "Anniversary"

Southern Poetry Review: "The Campesino's Lament," "Old Women," "How to Get a Baby," and "To a Daughter I Cannot Console"

Witness: The Paterson Public Library

A version of the folktale "The Witch's Husband," translated by Judith Ortiz Cofer, was first published by the Pig Iron Press Anthology of Third World Writers, 1988.

The author also expresses her gratitude to the National Endowment for the Arts, the Georgia Council for the Arts, and the Witter Bynner Foundation for Poetry for their support during the years when many of the works in this book were written. Thanks also to Rafael Ocasio, Edna Acosta-Belén, and Madelaine Cooke; to Malcolm Call and Karen Orchard, for their guidance and encouragement; and also, as always, to John Cofer.

The Latin Deli

The Latin Deli: An Ars Poetica

Presiding over a formica counter,
plastic Mother and Child magnetized
to the top of an ancient register,
the heady mix of smells from the open bins
of dried codfish, the green plantains
hanging in stalks like votive offerings,
she is the Patroness of Exiles,
a woman of no-age who was never pretty,
who spends her days selling canned memories
while listening to the Puerto Ricans complain
that it would be cheaper to fly to San Juan
than to buy a pound of Bustelo coffee here,
and to Cubans perfecting their speech
of a "glorious return" to Havana—where no one
has been allowed to die and nothing to change until then;
to Mexicans who pass through, talking lyrically
of *dólares* to be made in El Norte—
                                  all wanting the comfort
of spoken Spanish, to gaze upon the family portrait
of her plain wide face, her ample bosom
resting on her plump arms, her look of maternal interest
as they speak to her and each other
of their dreams and their disillusions—
how she smiles understanding,
when they walk down the narrow aisles of her store
reading the labels of packages aloud, as if
they were the names of lost lovers: *Suspiros,*
Merengues, the stale candy of everyone's childhood.

                                        She spends her days
slicing *jamón y queso* and wrapping it in wax paper
tied with string: plain ham and cheese
that would cost less at the A&P, but it would not satisfy
the hunger of the fragile old man lost in the folds
of his winter coat, who brings her lists of items
that he reads to her like poetry, or the others,
whose needs she must divine, conjuring up products
from places that now exist only in their hearts—
closed ports she must trade with.

FROM THE BOOK OF DREAMS IN SPANISH

Para venir a lo que no sabes,
has de ir por donde no sabes.

— San Juan de la Cruz

To come to what you do not know,
you must go by the way you do not know.

— St. John of the Cross

American History

I once read in a *Ripley's Believe It or Not* column that Paterson, New Jersey, is the place where the Straight and Narrow (streets) intersect. The Puerto Rican tenement known as El Building was one block up from Straight. It was, in fact, the corner of Straight and Market; not "at" the corner, but *the* corner. At almost any hour of the day, El Building was like a monstrous jukebox, blasting out *salsas* from open windows as the residents, mostly new immigrants just up from the island, tried to drown out whatever they were currently enduring with loud music. But the day President Kennedy was shot, there was a profound silence in El Building, even the abusive tongues of viragoes, the cursing of the unemployed, and the screeching of small children had been somehow muted. President Kennedy was a saint to these people. In fact, soon his photograph would be hung alongside the Sacred Heart and over the spiritist altars that many women kept in their apartments. He would become part of the hierarchy of martyrs they prayed to for favors that only one who had died for a cause would understand.

On the day that President Kennedy was shot, my ninth grade class had been out in the fenced playground of Public School Number 13. We had been given "free" exercise time and had been ordered by our P.E. teacher, Mr. DePalma, to "keep moving." That meant that the girls should jump rope and the boys toss basketballs through a hoop at the far end of the yard. He in the meantime would "keep an eye" on us from just inside the building.

It was a cold gray day in Paterson. The kind that warns of early snow. I was miserable, since I had forgotten my gloves and my knuckles were turning red and raw from the jump rope. I was also taking a lot of abuse from the black girls for not turning the rope hard and fast enough for them.

7

"Hey, Skinny Bones, pump it, girl. Ain't you got no energy today?" Gail, the biggest of the black girls who had the other end of the rope yelled, "Didn't you eat your rice and beans and pork chops for breakfast today?"

The other girls picked up the "pork chop" and made it into a refrain: "pork chop, pork chop, did you eat your pork chop?" They entered the double ropes in pairs and exited without tripping or missing a beat. I felt a burning on my cheeks, and then my glasses fogged up so that I could not manage to coordinate the jump rope with Gail. The chill was doing to me what it always did, entering my bones, making me cry, humiliating me. I hated the city, especially in winter. I hated Public School Number 13. I hated my skinny flat-chested body, and I envied the black girls who could jump rope so fast that their legs became a blur. They always seemed to be warm while I froze.

There was only one source of beauty and light for me that school year. The only thing I had anticipated at the start of the semester. That was seeing Eugene. In August, Eugene and his family had moved into the only house on the block that had a yard and trees. I could see his place from my window in El Building. In fact, if I sat on the fire escape I was literally suspended above Eugene's backyard. It was my favorite spot to read my library books in the summer. Until that August the house had been occupied by an old Jewish couple. Over the years I had become part of their family, without their knowing it, of course. I had a view of their kitchen and their backyard, and though I could not hear what they said, I knew when they were arguing, when one of them was sick, and many other things. I knew all this by watching them at mealtimes. I could see their kitchen table, the sink and the stove. During good times, he sat at the table and read his newspapers while she fixed the meals. If they argued, he would leave and the old woman would sit and stare at nothing for a long time. When one of them was sick, the other would come and get things from the kitchen and carry them out on a tray. The old man had died in June. The last week of school I had not seen

8

him at the table at all. Then one day I saw that there was a crowd in the kitchen. The old woman had finally emerged from the house on the arm of a stocky middle-aged woman whom I had seen there a few times before, maybe her daughter. Then a man had carried out suitcases. The house had stood empty for weeks. I had had to resist the temptation to climb down into the yard and water the flowers the old lady had taken such good care of.

By the time Eugene's family moved in, the yard was a tangled mass of weeds. The father had spent several days mowing, and when he finished, I didn't see the red, yellow, and purple clusters that meant flowers to me from where I sat. I didn't see this family sit down at the kitchen table together. It was just the mother, a red-headed tall woman who wore a white uniform—a nurse's, I guessed it was; the father was gone before I got up in the morning and was never there at dinner time. I only saw him on weekends when they sometimes sat on lawn chairs under the oak tree, each hidden behind a section of the newspaper; and there was Eugene. He was tall and blond, and he wore glasses. I liked him right away because he sat at the kitchen table and read books for hours. That summer, before we had even spoken one word to each other, I kept him company on my fire escape.

Once school started I looked for him in all my classes, but P.S. 13 was a huge, overpopulated place and it took me days and many discreet questions to discover that Eugene was in honors classes for all his subjects; classes that were not open to me because English was not my first language, though I was a straight A student. After much maneuvering I managed "to run into him" in the hallway where his locker was—on the other side of the building from mine—and in study hall at the library, where he first seemed to notice me but did not speak; and finally, on the way home after school one day when I decided to approach him directly, though my stomach was doing somersaults.

I was ready for rejection, snobbery, the worst. But when I came up to him, practically panting in my nervousness, and blurted out: "You're Eugene. Right?" He smiled, pushed his glasses up on his

9

nose, and nodded. I saw then that he was blushing deeply. Eugene liked me, but he was shy. I did most of the talking that day. He nodded and smiled a lot. In the weeks that followed, we walked home together. He would linger at the corner of El Building for a few minutes then walk down to his two-story house. It was not until Eugene moved into that house that I noticed that El Building blocked most of the sun and that the only spot that got a little sunlight during the day was the tiny square of earth the old woman had planted with flowers.

I did not tell Eugene that I could see inside his kitchen from my bedroom. I felt dishonest, but I liked my secret sharing of his evenings, especially now that I knew what he was reading, since we chose our books together at the school library.

One day my mother came into my room as I was sitting on the windowsill staring out. In her abrupt way she said: "Elena, you are acting 'moony.'" *Enamorada* was what she really said—that is, like a girl stupidly infatuated. Since I had turned fourteen and started menstruating my mother had been more vigilant than ever. She acted as if I was going to go crazy or explode or something if she didn't watch me and nag me all the time about being a señorita now. She kept talking about virtue, morality, and other subjects that did not interest me in the least. My mother was unhappy in Paterson, but my father had a good job at the blue jeans factory in Passaic, and soon, he kept assuring us, we would be moving to our own house there. Every Sunday we drove out to the suburbs of Paterson, Clifton, and Passaic, out to where people mowed grass on Sundays in the summer and where children made snowmen in the winter from pure white snow, not like the gray slush of Paterson, which seemed to fall from the sky in that hue. I had learned to listen to my parents' dreams, which were spoken in Spanish, as fairy tales, like the stories about life in the island paradise of Puerto Rico before I was born. I had been to the Island once as a little girl, to grandmother's funeral, and all I remembered was wailing women in black, my mother becoming hysterical and being given a pill that made her sleep two days, and me feeling lost in a crowd of strangers all claiming to be my aunts, uncles, and cousins. I had actually been glad to return to the city. We had not been back there since then, though my parents talked constantly about buying a house on the beach someday, retiring on the island—that was a common topic among the residents of El Building. As for me, I was going to go to college and become a teacher.

But after meeting Eugene I began to think of the present more than of the future. What I wanted now was to enter that house I had watched for so many years. I wanted to see the other rooms where the old people had lived and where the boy I liked spent his time. Most of all, I wanted to sit at the kitchen table with Eugene like two adults, like the old man and his wife had done, maybe drink some coffee and talk about books. I had started reading *Gone with the Wind*. I was enthralled by it, with the daring and the passion of the beautiful girl living in a mansion, and with her devoted parents and the slaves who did everything for them. I didn't believe such a world had ever really existed, and I wanted to ask Eugene some questions, since he and his parents, he had told me, had come up from Georgia, the same place where the novel was set. His father worked for a company that had transferred him to Paterson. His mother was very unhappy, Eugene said, in his beautiful voice that rose and fell over words in a strange, lilting way. The kids at school called him the Hick and made fun of the way he talked. I knew I was his only friend so far, and I liked that, though I felt sad for him sometimes. Skinny Bones and the Hick, was what they called us at school when we were seen together.

The day Mr. DePalma came out into the cold and asked us to line up in front of him was the day that President Kennedy was shot. Mr. DePalma, a short, muscular man with slicked-down black hair, was the science teacher, P.E. coach, and disciplinarian at P.S. 13. He was the teacher to whose homeroom you got assigned if you were a troublemaker, and the man called out to break up playground fights, and to escort violently angry teenagers to the office. And Mr. De-Palma was the man who called your parents in for "a conference."

That day, he stood in front of two rows of mostly black and Puerto

Rican kids, brittle from their efforts to "keep moving" on a November day that was turning bitter cold. Mr. DePalma, to our complete shock, was crying. Not just silent adult tears, but really sobbing. There were a few titters from the back of the line where I stood, shivering.

"Listen," Mr. DePalma raised his arms over his head as if he were about to conduct an orchestra. His voice broke, and he covered his face with his hands. His barrel chest was heaving. Someone giggled behind me.

"Listen," he repeated, "something awful has happened." A strange gurgling came from his throat, and he turned around and spit on the cement behind him.

"Gross," someone said, and there was a lot of laughter.

"The president is dead, you idiots. I should have known that wouldn't mean anything to a bunch of losers like you kids. Go home." He was shrieking now. No one moved for a minute or two, but then a big girl let out a "yeah!" and ran to get her books piled up with the others against the brick wall of the school building. The others followed in a mad scramble to get to their things before somebody caught on. It was still an hour to the dismissal bell.

A little scared, I headed for El Building. There was an eerie feeling on the streets. I looked into Mario's drugstore, a favorite hangout for the high school crowd, but there were only a couple of old Jewish men at the soda bar, talking with the short order cook in tones that sounded almost angry, but they were keeping their voices low. Even the traffic on one of the busiest intersections in Paterson—Straight Street and Park Avenue—seemed to be moving slower. There were no horns blasting that day. At El Building, the usual little group of unemployed men were not hanging out on the front stoop, making it difficult for women to enter the front door. No music spilled out from open doors in the hallway. When I walked into our apartment, I found my mother sitting in front of the grainy picture of the television set.

She looked up at me with a tear-streaked face and just said: "Dios mío," turning back to the set as if it were pulling at her eyes. I went into my room.

Though I wanted to feel the right thing about President Kennedy's death, I could not fight the feeling of elation that stirred in my chest. Today was the day I was to visit Eugene in his house. He had asked me to come over after school to study for an American history test with him. We had also planned to walk to the public library together. I looked down into his yard. The oak tree was bare of leaves, and the ground looked gray with ice. The light through the large kitchen window of his house told me that El Building blocked the sun to such an extent that they had to turn lights on in the middle of the day. I felt ashamed about it. But the white kitchen table with the lamp hanging just above it looked cozy and inviting. I would soon sit there, across from Eugene, and I would tell him about my perch just above his house. Maybe I would.

In the next thirty minutes I changed clothes, put on a little pink lipstick, and got my books together. Then I went in to tell my mother that I was going to a friend's house to study. I did not expect her reaction.

"You are going out *today?*" The way she said "today" sounded as if a storm warning had been issued. It was said in utter disbelief. Before I could answer, she came toward me and held my elbows as I clutched my books.

"*Hija*, the president has been killed. We must show respect. He was a great man. Come to church with me tonight."

She tried to embrace me, but my books were in the way. My first impulse was to comfort her, she seemed so distraught, but I had to meet Eugene in fifteen minutes.

"I have a test to study for, Mama. I will be home by eight."

"You are forgetting who you are, *Niña*. I have seen you staring down at that boy's house. You are heading for humiliation and pain." My mother said this in Spanish and in a resigned tone that surprised me, as if she had no intention of stopping me from "heading for humiliation and pain." I started for the door. She sat in front of the TV, holding a white handkerchief to her face.

I walked out to the street and around the chain-link fence that separated El Building from Eugene's house. The yard was neatly edged around the little walk that led to the door. It always amazed me how Paterson, the inner core of the city, had no apparent logic to its architecture. Small, neat, single residences like this one could be found right next to huge, dilapidated apartment buildings like El Building. My guess was that the little houses had been there first, then the immigrants had come in droves, and the monstrosities had been raised for them—the Italians, the Irish, the Jews, and now us, the Puerto Ricans, and the blacks. The door was painted a deep green: *verde*, the color of hope. I had heard my mother say it: *Verde-Esperanza*.

I knocked softly. A few suspenseful moments later the door opened just a crack. The red, swollen face of a woman appeared. She had a halo of red hair floating over a delicate ivory face—the face of a doll—with freckles on the nose. Her smudged eye makeup made her look unreal to me, like a mannequin seen through a warped store window.

"What do you want?" Her voice was tiny and sweet-sounding, like a little girl's, but her tone was not friendly.

"I'm Eugene's friend. He asked me over. To study." I thrust out my books, a silly gesture that embarrassed me almost immediately.

"You live there?" She pointed up to El Building, which looked particularly ugly, like a gray prison with its many dirty windows and rusty fire escapes. The woman had stepped halfway out, and I could see that she wore a white nurse's uniform with "St. Joseph's Hospital" on the name tag.

"Yes. I do."

She looked intently at me for a couple of heartbeats, then said as if to herself, "I don't know how you people do it." Then directly to me: "Listen. Honey. Eugene doesn't want to study with you. He is a smart boy. Doesn't need help. You understand me. I am truly sorry

14

if he told you you could come over. He cannot study with you. It's nothing personal. You understand? We won't be in this place much longer, no need for him to get close to people—it'll just make it harder for him later. Run back home now."

I couldn't move. I just stood there in shock at hearing these things said to me in such a honey-drenched voice. I had never heard an accent like hers except for Eugene's softer version. It was as if she were singing me a little song.

"What's wrong? Didn't you hear what I said?" She seemed very angry, and I finally snapped out of my trance. I turned away from the green door and heard her close it gently.

Our apartment was empty when I got home. My mother was in someone else's kitchen, seeking the solace she needed. Father would come in from his late shift at midnight. I would hear them talking softly in the kitchen for hours that night. They would not discuss their dreams for the future, or life in Puerto Rico, as they often did; that night they would talk sadly about the young widow and her two children, as if they were family. For the next few days, we would observe *luto* in our apartment; that is, we would practice restraint and silence—no loud music or laughter. Some of the women of El Building would wear black for weeks.

That night, I lay in my bed, trying to feel the right thing for our dead president. But the tears that came up from a deep source inside me were strictly for me. When my mother came to the door, I pretended to be sleeping. Sometime during the night, I saw from my bed the streetlight come on. It had a pink halo around it. I went to my window and pressed my face to the cool glass. Looking up at the light I could see the white snow falling like a lace veil over its face. I did not look down to see it turning gray as it touched the ground below.

Not for Sale

El Árabe was what the Puerto Rican women called him. He sold them beautiful things from his exotic homeland in the afternoons, at that hour when the day's work is done and there is a little time before the evening duties. He did not carry anything men would buy. His merchandise, mostly linens, was impractical but exquisite. The bed covers were gorgeously woven into oriental tales that he narrated to his customers in his halting Spanish. My mother bought the Scheherazade. It was expensive, but she desired it for my bed, since it was the year when I was being denied everything by my father: no dating like other sixteen-year-olds (I was a decent Puerto Rican señorita, not a wild American teenager); no driver's license (the streets of Paterson, New Jersey, were too dangerous for an inexperienced driver—he would take me where I needed to go); no end-of-the-school-year weekend trip with my junior class to Seaside Heights (even though three teachers would be chaperoning us). No, *no, no,* with a short Spanish "o." Final: no lingering vowels in my father's pronouncements.

She knew that I could be brought out of my surliness, my seething anger at my father's constant vigilance, by a visit from the storytelling salesman. On the days when I heard the heavy footfall on the staircase announcing his coming, I would emerge from my room, where I kept company only with my English-language books no one else in the house could read. Since I was not allowed to linger at the drugstore with my high school classmates nor to go out socially—unless my father could be persuaded to let me after interrogations and arguments I had come to dread—I had turned to reading in seclusion. Books kept me from going mad. They allowed me to imagine my circumstances as romantic: some days I was an Indian princess living in a *zenana*, a house of women, keeping myself pure, being trained for a brilliant future. Other days I was a prisoner: Papillon, preparing myself for my great flight to freedom. When El Árabe came to our door, bearing his immense stack of bed linens on his shoulder, I ran to let him in. Mother brought him a glass of cold water as he settled into a rocking chair. I sat on the linoleum floor Indian-style while he spread his merchandise in front of us. Sometimes he brought jewelry too. He carried the rings and bracelets in a little red velvet bag he pulled out of his coat pocket. The day he showed us the Scheherazade bedspread, he emptied the glittering contents of the velvet bag on my lap, then he took my hand and fitted a gold ring with an immense green stone on my finger. It was ornate and covered my finger up to the knuckle, scratching the tender skin in between fingers. Feeling nervous, I laughed and tried to take it off. But he shook his head no. He said that he wanted me to keep the ring on while he told me some of the stories woven on the bedspread. It was a magic ring, he said, that would help me understand. My mother gave me a little frown from the doorway behind El Árabe, meaning *Be polite but give it back soon.* El Árabe settled back to tell his stories. Every so often he would unfold another corner of the bedspread to illustrate a scene.

On a gold background with green threads running through it, glossy like the patina on the dome at city hall, the weavers had put the seated figure of the storytelling woman among the characters she had created. She seemed to be invisible to them. In each panel she sat slightly behind the action in the posture of wisdom, which the salesman demonstrated: mouth parted and arms extended toward her audience, like a Buddha or a sacred dancer. While Sinbad wields his sword at a pirate, Scheherazade sits calmly in between them. She can be found on the street corner, where Aladdin trades his new lamps for old. But he does not see her.

El Árabe spoke deliberately, but his Spanish was still difficult to understand. It was as if his tongue had trouble with certain of our sound combinations. But he was patient. When he saw that one of us had lost the thread of the story, he would begin again, sometimes at the beginning.

This usually drove my mother out of the room, but I understood that these tales were one continuous story to him. If broken, the pattern would be ruined. They had to be told all the way through. I looked at him closely as he spoke. He appeared to be about my father's age, but it was hard to tell, because a thick beard covered most of his face. His eyes revealed his fatigue. He was stooped from carrying his bundles from building to building, I assumed. No one seemed to know where he lived or whether he had a family. But on the day of the Scheherazade stories he told me about his son. The subject seemed to arise naturally out of the last tale. The king who beheaded his brides was captivated by the storytelling woman and spared her life. I felt uneasy with this ending, though I had read it before, not trusting the gluttonous King Shahryar to keep his word. And what would happen to Scheherazade when she ran out of stories? It was always the same with these fairy tales: the plot was fascinating, but the ending was unsatisfactory to me. "Happily ever after" was a loose knot tied on a valuable package.

El Árabe took the first payment on the bedspread from my mother who had, I knew, gotten the dollar bills out of her underwear drawer where she kept her "secret" little stash of money in the foot of a nylon stocking. She probably thought that neither my father nor I would have any reason to look there. But in that year of my seclusion, nothing was safe from my curiosity: if I could not go out and explore the world, I would learn what I could from within the four walls. Sometimes I was Anne Frank, and what little there was to discover from my keepers belonged by rights to me.

She counted out ten dollars slowly into his hand. He opened his little notebook with frayed pages. He wrote with a pencil: the full amount at the top, her name, the date, and "10.00" with a flourish. She winced a little as she followed his numbers. It would take her a long time to pay it off. She asked me if I really wanted it—three times. But she knew what it meant to me.

My mother left with the bedspread, explaining that she wanted to see how it would look on my bed. El Árabe seemed reluctant to leave. He lit a slender, aromatic cigarette he took out of a gold case with a little diamond in the middle. Then he repeated the story of Scheherazade's winning over of her husband. Though I was by now weary of the repetition, I listened politely. It was then that he said that he had a son, a handsome young man who wanted very much to come to America to take over the business. There was much money to be made. I nodded, not really understanding why he was telling me all this.

But I fell under the spell of his words as he described a heroic vision of a handsome man who rode thoroughbreds over a golden desert. Without my being aware of it, the afternoon passed quickly. It caught me entirely by surprise when I heard the key turning in the front door lock. I was really chagrined at being found out of my room by my father.

He walked in on us before I had time to rise from my childish position on the floor at El Árabe's feet.

He came in, smelling strongly of sweat and coffee from the factory where he was the watchman. I never understood why sacks of un-processed coffee beans had to be watched, but that's all I knew about his job. He walked in, looking annoyed and suspicious. He did not like any interruption of his routines: he wanted to find my mother and me in our places when he came home. If she had a friend drop by, Mother had to make sure the visit ended before he arrived. I had stopped inviting my friends over after a while, since his silent hostility made them uncomfortable. Long ago, when I was a little girl, he had spent hours every evening playing with me and reading to me in Spanish. Now, since those activities no longer appealed to me, since I wanted to spend time with other people, he showed no interest in me, except to say no to my requests for permission to go out.

Mother tried to mediate between us by reminding me often of my father's early affection. She explained that teenage girls in Puerto Rico did not go out without chaperons as I wanted to do. They stayed home and helped their mothers and obeyed their fathers. Didn't he give me everything I needed?

I had felt furious at her absurd statements. They did not apply to me, or to the present reality of my life in Paterson, New Jersey. I would work myself into a shouting frenzy. I would scream out my protests that we were not living in some backward country where women were slaves.

"Look," I would point out of the window of our fifth-story apartment in a building at the core of the city. "Do you see palm trees, any sand or blue water? All I see is concrete. We are in the United States. I am an American citizen. I speak English better than Spanish and I am as old as you were when you got married!" The arguments would end with her in tears and the heavy blanket of angry silence falling over both of us. It was no use talking to him either. He had her to comfort him for the unfairness of twelve-hour days in a factory and for being too tired to do anything else but read *La Prensa* in the evenings. I felt like an exile in the foreign country of my parents' house.

My father walked into the living room and immediately focused his eyes on the immense ring on my finger. Without greeting the salesman, without acknowledging my mother who had just returned to the room, he kept pointing at my hand. El Árabe stood up and bowed his head to my father in a strange formal way. Then he said something very odd—something like *I greet you as a kinsman, the ring is a gift to your daughter from my son.* What followed was utter confusion. My father kept asking what? what? what? I struggled to my feet trying to remove the ring from my finger, but it seemed to be stuck. My mother waved me into the kitchen where we worked soap around the swollen finger. In silence we listened to the shouting match in the living room. Both men seemed to be talking at once.

From what I could make out, El Árabe was proposing to my father that I be sold to him—for a fair price—to be his son's bride. This was necessary, since his son could not immigrate quickly unless he married an American citizen. The old salesman was willing to bargain with my father over what I was worth in this transaction. I heard figures, a listing of merchandise, a certain number of cattle and horses his son could sell in their country for cash if that was what my father preferred.

My father seemed to be choking. He could not break through the expert haggler's multilingual stream of offers and descriptions of family wealth. My mother pulled the ring off my finger, scraping away some of the skin along with it. I tried not to cry out, but something broke in me when I heard my father's anguished scream of *Not for sale! Not for sale!* persisting until the salesman fell silent. My mother rushed the ring out to the living room while I tried to regain my self-control. But my father's hoarse voice repeating the one phrase echoed in my ears; even after there was the sound of a door being shut and the dull, heavy footsteps of a burdened man descending the stairs, I heard the pained protest.

Then my father came into the kitchen, where I was standing at the sink, washing the blood off my fingers. The ring had cut me deeply. He stood in silence and, unmoving in the doorway, looked at me as if he had not seen me in a long time or just then for the first time. Then he asked me in a soft voice if I was all right. I nodded, hiding my hand behind my back.

In the months that followed, my mother paid on her account at the door. El Árabe did not come into our apartment again. My father learned the word "yes" in English and practiced saying it occasionally, though "no" remained NO in both languages and easier to say for a nonnative speaker.

On my bed Scheherazade kept telling her stories, which I came to understand would never end—as I had once feared—since it was in my voice that she spoke to me, placing my dreams among hers, weaving them in.

Twist and Shout

It's 1967, summer, and I'm as restless as all of America. The Beatles are inundating the airwaves in our apartment building, drowning out our parents' salsas. My mother has left me alone to keep an eye on the red kidney beans boiling for dinner, while she goes to the bodega for orégano or some other ingredient she needs. She had tried in vain to make me understand what it is, but I have resisted her Spanish. As soon as she has gone down one flight of stairs, I run up two, to 5-B, where the music has been playing loud enough for me to hear from my room. The door is unlocked and I burst in on Manny dancing with his sister, Amelia, who is fifteen and wants to be called Amy. Amy's best friend Cecilia (Ceci) is stretched out on the sofa like Elizabeth Taylor in *Cleopatra*. They are all singing along with the Beatles' "Twist and Shout." Manny and Amy are dancing too close for brother and sister. They are grinding their bodies together, chest to chest and hip to hip.

I have a crush on Manny, who is Puerto Rican like me but has blue eyes and curly blond hair. His father was an American. Amy is dark like me: different fathers.

Manny suddenly grabs me from where I have flattened myself against the door to watch them dance. He's much taller than I am and too old to be in the eighth grade—fourteen. Their mother moves them from place to place in the city a lot, so they've both been held back a couple of grades. All the Puerto Rican girls are crazy about Manny. He's a great dancer, and there's a rumor—not a virgin. Manny pushes Amy away and wraps himself around me. I feel my heart pounding against my rib cage like when I jump double-Dutch-rope in the school playground. I'm using my arms and elbows against him, to try to get a little air between us. I want to get close to Manny but not so close that I can't breathe. I'm a little scared at the way his body is moving and his hot mouth is pressing on my head. He is singing along with John Lennon, and I feel every word on my skin, since his wet lips are traveling down my neck. I manage to twist my face away just as Lennon hits the high note, over his shoulder I see Amy and Ceci making out on the sofa. *They are kissing on the mouth.* Their faces are contorted into what looks like pain but what I have learned to recognize, from the Spanish TV soap operas my mother and I watch at night, as passion.

Manny has me pinned to the wall and is grinding his hips into mine. It hurts a little, since I'm skinny and my pelvic bones stick out, but it feels good too. I think this is what I came up to 5-B for but too much all at once. Suddenly I remember my mother's red kidney beans. I have a vision of them boiling down into a sticky, sour paste. That's what can happen if you don't watch them. The thought of what my mother would do gives me the strength I need to pry myself out of Manny's iron grasp. He springs away from me and into a spin like one of the Temptations—what a good dancer he is. He could be on TV. I watch him land on the tangle of arms and legs that are Amy and Ceci on the sofa. Like an octopus having a snack, they pull him down and engulf him.

I hear them laughing above the music and the group's throat-scraping final shout.

As I enter our kitchen, I smell the beans: almost done. Their shells will be tender but still intact. I add a little water—just to be on the safe side. Then, still feeling a little weak in the knees, I sit down at the table to watch them.

By Love Betrayed

As a little girl I imagined my father was a genie that came out of a magic bottle at night. It was a green bottle of cologne that he splashed on his face before leaving the house. I thought it was the strong smell that made my mother cry.

I loved him more than anyone. He was beautiful to me with his dark, shiny black hair combed back like one of the handsome men on the *telenovelas* my mother watched while she waited for him to come home at night. I was allowed to stay up for the early one: *Traicionado por el amor:* By Love Betrayed.

My *papi* had a mustache like a thin brush that tickled me when he kissed me. If they had not been shouting at each other, he would sometimes come into my room and say good-night before he left for his job at the nightclub. Then his perfume would get on my blanket and I would hold it to my face until I fell asleep. I dreamed of him and me walking on a beach. I had never been to the ocean, but he told me stories about growing up in a house on the beach in Puerto Rico. It had been blown away by a hurricane.

When my mother got angry at my father, she made me think of a hurricane. Blowing him away from us with her screams and her tears. Once, she scratched his cheek. He covered it with her makeup before he left for work. Another time I heard a sound like a slap, but I did not know who hit whom, because my mother always cried, and he always left.

Sometimes I would hear her saying the rosary aloud, the dozens of Hail Marys and Our Fathers was a song that would put me to sleep better than any lullaby. She had come back to the church after leaving it when she had run away with Papi. My mother said that Tito had taken her away from God but that now she was back to stay. She had the priest come to our apartment and sprinkle it with holy water, which doesn't smell like anything.

My mother made our apartment look like a church too: she put a cross with Christ on it over their bed and mine—Papi liked to say that one day it would fall on their heads and kill them, and my mother would answer, "Well, Tito, I'm ready to go to my Dios any time, are you?" He would just laugh. She hung a picture of the Holy Mother and Baby Jesus on the wall facing my bed, and one of Christ knocking at a door in the hallway. On her dresser she had a painted statue of the Virgin Mary crushing a black snake. When you saw it on the mirror it looked as if she was a real little person who was about to trip over a snake because she wasn't looking where she was going. I used to play pretend and try to take the snake out. But it was glued on under her little foot. My mother did not like me to play with the saint dolls, though, and I had to sneak into their room when she was busy in the kitchen or watching TV.

My parents argued a lot. Our apartment was small, and I heard them saying the same things over and over in as many different hurting words as was possible. I learned my fighting words in Spanish then: the words to hurt and also the words of the church that my mother taught me so that I would not turn out a sinner like my father.

"Who made you?"

"God made me."

"Why did He make you?"

"To glorify His Name and to obey His commands and those of His Church."

We said this lesson over and over in our catechism class with Sister Teresa who was preparing us for First Communion.

When I got older, I tried to ask my mother questions about my father. Her answers were always the same:

"Where does Papi go at night?"

"To his job."

"But he has a job during the day. He's the super of our building, right?"

"He has two jobs. Finish your cereal. It's getting late for school."

When she made up her mind not to talk about my father, I could not make her say a word. For many years I could not talk to him, since the only time he was at home, in between his jobs, she was also there, watching me. Finally I got my chance to see my papi alone after she started volunteer work at the church several mornings a week when I was in third grade.

One day she had to leave early to help plan a women's religious retreat. She put a bowl of cereal in front of me and told me to walk carefully to school. I was big enough to walk the four blocks alone, especially since there were crossing guards at every corner. I kissed her good-bye and asked for my blessing: "Dios te bendiga, Hija," she said and crossed herself.

"Amén," I said and crossed myself.

I ran to the living room window from where I could see her come out on the street and walk toward the church. After she disappeared around the corner, I took the house key and left our apartment to look for my father. I was not sure what I would do when I found him. I felt scared and excited, though, knowing that I was doing something that would make my mother angry if she found out. I knew that Papi would not tell.

It was a big building with long dark hallways that wound around each other for seven floors. I had never been above our third floor. When I reached the fifth floor, I smelled his cologne. I followed it to the door of 5-A. I knew for sure that he was somewhere near because his toolbox was in the corner of the landing. I stood in front of the door with my knees shaking, afraid to knock and afraid to turn back. The building was quiet at that hour. All the children were in school and most people at work. I put my head to the door and listened.

First I heard a woman's voice saying my father's name in a strange way: "Tito, Tito . . ." She said it as if they were playing a game. Then I heard his voice, but I could not understand the words. Then they both laughed. I decided to knock.

The woman who opened the door was wearing a red robe and her hair was a mess. Her lipstick was purple. I remember thinking that she looked like a vampire. I felt like running away, especially since she looked a little wild with her blonde-streaked hair all over her face. She had dark skin and blonde-streaked hair. I remember that.

"What do you want?" she said in an angry voice.

"I . . . I'm looking for my father."

"Your *father?*" She looked behind her. He had come out of her bedroom. I knew it was her bedroom because her apartment was just like ours, except for the furniture. Her sofa was black, and she had no curtains on her windows. My father was combing his hair with the black comb he always carried in his shirt pocket. He looked really surprised to see me at the door.

"Eva, what are you doing here?" Before I could answer, though, he closed the door behind him—right on the woman's face. I was really nervous. I couldn't tell him what I was doing there because I didn't know myself. He bent down and looked at me. He looked nervous too. I could tell because his left eye twitched when he was upset; I've seen it do that after he and my mother had a fight. "Are you sick, Evita? Why aren't you at school? Where is your mother?" He looked around as if he thought she was behind me somewhere.

"I stayed home, Papi. I had a headache. She's gone to church." He had been squeezing my shoulder with his hand, but he let go of me then. He smiled in a way my mother called his "devil smile." She said that meant he thought he knew it all. That nobody could fool him. He claimed that he always knew when somebody had a secret around the house. And that's how he found the money she had been saving behind her underwear drawer.

"Are you really sick or just taking the day off, *mi amor?*"

I just smiled, trying for a "devil smile" myself.

"I thought so. Well, maybe I'll do the same. The señora's clogged sink can wait another day. How about a hamburger at the White Castle for lunch?"

"It's only 9:30, Papi. Not time for lunch."

"Says who? Today *we* decide everything by ourselves. Deal?" He gave me his hand and I took it.

From "Some Spanish Verbs"

Orar: To Pray

After the hissed pleas, denunciations—
the children just tucked in—
perhaps her hand on his dress-shirt sleeve,
brushed off, leaving a trace of cologne,
impossible, it seemed, to wash off
with plain soap, he'd go, his feet light
on the gravel. In their room, she'd fall
on her knees to say prayers composed
to sound like praise; following
her mother's warning never to make demands
outright from God nor a man.

On the other side of the thin wall,
I lay listening to the sounds I recognized
from an early age: Knees on wood, shifting
the pain so the floor creaked, and a woman's
conversation with the wind—that carried
her sad voice out of the open window
to me. And her words—if they did not rise
to heaven, fell on my chest, where they are
embedded like splinters of a cross

I also carried.

Dividir: To Divide

After the rumors about the fake-blonde widow
next door, she chose pride; he, humility.
That was twenty years before he died
surrounded by his children and all the others
who loved the old man—silenced long before
by a woman's cold eyes.

She chose pride. She would accept
no help hauling groceries, small children,
and whatever load she carried home
up that steep hill to the house
they had in common. He would try at first,
hands outstretched like Christ's helper
in the fifth station of the cross.
But she preferred pain to compromise.

He chose humility. And it worked.
The grandchildren, accustomed to the rages
of women, saw our tiny selves reflected
in his sad eyes, punished like him
beyond our petty crimes; in her hard gaze,
there was a stone husband, frozen
in the act. We watched her work
in fury, cook the endless meals, press
his clothes as if his back were on the board,
each slam of the iron making it quiver
on its thin legs.

When he fell ill, she stood guard
in the hall outside his room, forbearing
all night on a straight-back chair,

directing the flow of doctors and despairing kin
with the calm eyes of a sphinx. And finally,
alone with him—did she catch his last breath
and hold it in her lungs until
she absorbed the soul of a man
who would never again wander?

I heard that she had kissed him
when he was gone. Then, kneeling by the bed,
washed and anointed his still body.
Taking it back.

Respirar: To Breathe

Seven years old, I had only
to cross the street from my second grade
classroom to my grandmother's house.
This day I saw the line snaking
into old Don Juan de Dios's living room.
A giveaway, I thought, remembering
the day the old man with a beard
that hung down to his huge middle
made snow cones for all of us
on a sweltering July day in Puerto Rico.
We had been allowed to run free
through a house saturated with old-age smells
and filled with treasures
from the world before our births.

It was a silent queue I joined, in between
women in black, I could only follow
the current into the flower-packed room
where Don Juan lay as still as I tried to be
in hide-and-seek. He seemed to be asleep.
When it was my turn to look, I stared
at his hands folded on his chest
and waited—no one tried to stop me
when I ran through the stifling crowd
and out to the air-filled world.

Volar: To Fly

  I have always known
that you will visit my grave.
I see myself as a small brown bird,
perhaps a sparrow, watching you
from a low branch as you pray
in front of my name.
  I will hear you
sound out my epitaph: *Aquí descansa
una mujer que quiso volar.*
You will recall telling me
that you once dreamed in Spanish,
and felt the words
lift you into flight.
  The sound of wings
will startle you when you say "volar,"
and you will understand.

An Early Mystery

Six years old,
I'm lingering over the candy counter.
On the other side of the bodega
my mother is interrogating the grocer
about the freshness of the produce:
the breadfruit, the yuccas, the plantains.
She does not trust him, I can tell.
I recognize the voice she uses
from listening late at night
when my father's late arrival
makes her sound that way: like a radio
picking up a faint signal,
then losing it.
                        Sometimes,
he comes in to kiss me, while I pretend
to sleep; but there are nights
when I hear the door click shut again.

Though involved in my task
of deciding over chocolate-covered coconut bars
that I can make last, or the bubble gum
wrapped in tiny English-language comic strips
that he can translate for me later,
I smell the woman approaching: familiar scent
of gardenias, cinnamon, alcohol—
my daddy's shirt and his breath
when he leans over my bed.
                        She stares at me
as in a trance, kneels down to look into my eyes.

Embarrassed, I hang my head, notice a run
racing up her stockinged knee toward her plump thigh
like a little jet on a tan sky, until it vanishes
under her tight black dress.

Are you his little girl?

                         Suddenly,
Mother is between us, pulling me away
before I can answer, or make my choice
of sweets.

I hear her walking toward the street, high heels
firing back at us like cap guns. On the aisle
where Mother and I stand holding hands,
there is something in the air so strong—
we could have followed it with closed eyes
all the way home.

Fever

In my childhood, father was to her and me
like the wind—blowing through our house on weekend leaves—
and when we spoke to him,
he carried our voices away with him.

He would leave Mother absorbed in a silence that grew
within her like a new pregnancy: I remember watching her
set the dinner table for two, then eat by herself
in the kitchen, standing.

Living with her taught me this:
That silence is a thick and dark curtain,
the kind that pulls down over a shop window;
that love is the repercussion of a stone
bouncing off that same window—and that pain
is something you can embrace, like a rag doll
nobody will ask you to share.

On the nights when she allowed me in her wide bed,
I'd lay my head close to hers—her skin was as cool
as the surface of the pillow the sick child clings to
between feverish dreams; and I'd listen to the delicate
knotted thread of her breathing—her rosary of sighs,
absorbing through my pores a sorrow so sweet
and sustaining that I lived on it,
as simply as the houseplant that adapts
to what light filters into a windowless room.

The Lesson of the Sugarcane

My mother opened her eyes wide
at the edge of the field
ready for cutting.
"Take a deep breath,"
                    she whispered,
"There is nothing as sweet:
Nada más dulce."
                    Overhearing,
Father left the flat he was changing
in the road-warping sun,
and grabbing my arm, broke my sprint
toward a stalk:
"Cane can choke a little girl: snakes hide
where it grows over your head."

And he led us back to the crippled car
where we sweated out our penitence,
for having craved more sweetness
than we were allowed,
more than we could handle.

A Legion of Dark Angels

They came down from the Sierra Maestra,
from its dizzying heights, wearing
the green of the forest, shouting prophecy:
those dusty dominions, those archangels
in full armor, nearly floating
through the ecstatic crowd—their bearded leader
sad and proud as the rejected Messiah
finally entering his Jerusalem.

Called in from play to witness
Cuba's liberation on our grainy TV screen,
we heard our father quote a poem
in Spanish he remembered from school,
a line about Puerto Rico and Cuba being—
De un pájaro, las dos alas—
of the same bird, its two wings.
And because he had been to Havana,
and had called it "Batista's Whore,"
he said "God bless Fidel," instructing us
to look upon a hero's face, and Mother,
crying softly for the sons and the brothers
who had not returned, kept saying: "Amen,
amen."

The Changeling

As a young girl
vying for my father's attention,
I invented a game that made him look up
from his reading and shake his head
as if both baffled and amused.

In my brother's closet, I'd change
into his dungarees—the rough material
molding me into boy shape; hide
my long hair under an army helmet
he'd been given by Father, and emerge
transformed into the legendary Che
of grown-up talk.

Strutting around the room,
I'd tell of life in the mountains,
of carnage and rivers of blood,
and of manly feasts with rum and music
to celebrate victories *para la libertad*.
He would listen with a smile
to my tales of battles and brotherhood
until Mother called us to dinner.

She was not amused
by my transformations, sternly forbidding me
from sitting down with them as a man.
She'd order me back to the dark cubicle
that smelled of adventure, to shed
my costume, to braid my hair furiously
with blind hands, and to return invisible,
as myself,
to the real world of her kitchen.

Absolution in the New Year

The decade is over, time to begin forgiving
old sins. Thirteen years since your death
on a Florida interstate—and again
a dream of an old wrong. Last night as I slept
through the turning of the year,
                            I was fifteen
and back on the day I hated you most: when
in a patriarchal fury at my sullen
keeping of myself to myself,
and convinced I was turning into a Jezebel,
you searched my room for evidence
of a secret other life. You found my diary
under the mattress and, taking it to the kitchen,
examined it under harsh light.
                        You read
about my childish fantasies of flight—yes—
from your tyrannical vigilance
and, in the last few pages, of my first love,
almost all imagination.
                      I suffered
biblical torments as you turned the pages. Unworthy,
exposed before your eyes, I wondered where
I would go, if you should cast me out
of your garden of thorns, but I swore, that day,
my faith to the inviolable self.
                      Later,
when Mother came in to offer me
a cup of consolation tea, her vague justifications
of "man's ways," and to return the profaned book,
I tore and crumpled each page, and left them
on the floor for her to sweep.

To this day
I cannot leave my notebooks open anywhere:
and I hide my secrets in poems.

A new year begins.
I am almost your age. And I can almost understand
your anger then—caught as you were—in a poor man's trap,
you needed to own, at least our souls.
For this sin of pride, I absolve you, Father.

And more:
If I could travel to your grave today,
I'd take my books of poetry as an offering
to your starved spirit
that fed on my dreams in those days.

I'd place poems on your stone marker,
over the part of your name we share,
over the brief span of your years (1933–1976),
like a Chinese daughter who brings a bowl of rice
and a letter to set on fire—a message
to be delivered by the wind: Father,

here is more for you to read.
Take all you desire of my words. Read
until you've had your fill.
Then rest in peace.

There is more where this came from.

From the Book of Dreams in Spanish

From the top branches
of the tamarind tree
into my outstretched hands
fell brown fruit, ripe
and sweeter than anything
I had ever tasted.

Ravenous,
I ate it all, catching it
before it touched the ground
where it vanished.

The book of dreams in Spanish
says the tree is my father.
The fruit that disappears
stands for words not spoken,
hopes and wishes left unfulfilled.
But it does not tell me
why I still feel starved
after I eat.

The Witch's Husband

My grandfather has misplaced his words again. He is trying to find my name in the kaleidoscope of images that his mind has become. His face brightens like a child's who has just remembered his lesson. He points to me and says my mother's name. I smile back and kiss him on the cheek. It doesn't matter what names he remembers anymore. Every day he is more confused, his memory slipping back a little further in time. Today he has no grandchildren yet. Tomorrow he will be a young man courting my grandmother again, quoting bits of poetry to her. In months to come, he will begin calling her Mamá.

I have traveled to Puerto Rico at my mother's request to help her deal with the old people. My grandfather is physically healthy, but his dementia is severe. My grandmother's heart is making odd sounds again in her chest. Yet she insists on taking care of the old man at home herself. She will not give up her house, though she has been warned that her heart might fail in her sleep without proper monitoring, that is, a nursing home or a relative's care. Her response is typical of her famous obstinacy: "*Bueno,*" she says, "I will die in my own bed."

I am now at her house, waiting for my opportunity to talk "sense" into her. As a college teacher in the United States I am supposed to represent the voice of logic; I have been called in to convince *la abuela*, the family's proud matriarch, to step down—to allow her children to take care of her before she kills herself with work. I spent years at her house as a child but have lived in the U.S. for most of my adult life. I learned to love and respect this strong woman, who with five children of her own had found a way to help many others. She was a legend in the pueblo for having more foster children than anyone else. I have spoken with people my mother's age who told me that they had spent up to a year at Abuela's house during emergencies and hard times. It seems extraordinary that a woman would willingly take on such obligations. And frankly, I am a bit appalled at what I have begun to think of as "the martyr complex" in Puerto Rican women, that is, the idea that self-sacrifice is a woman's lot and her privilege: a good woman is defined by how much suffering and mothering she can do in one lifetime. Abuela is the all-time champion in my eyes: her life has been entirely devoted to others. Not content to bring up two sons and three daughters as the Depression raged on, followed by the war that took one of her sons, she had also taken on other people's burdens. This had been the usual pattern with one exception that I knew of: the year that Abuela spent in New York, apparently undergoing some kind of treatment for her heart while she was still a young woman. My mother was five or six years old, and there were three other children who had been born by that time too. They were given into the care of Abuela's sister, Delia. The two women traded places for the year. Abuela went to live in her sister's apartment in New York City while the younger woman took over Abuela's duties at the house in Puerto Rico. Grandfather was a shadowy figure in the background during that period. My mother doesn't say much about what went on during that year, only that her mother was sick and away for months. Grandfather seemed absent too, since he worked all of the time. Though they missed Abuela, they were well taken care of.

I am sitting on a rocking chair on the porch of her house. She is facing me from a hammock she made when her first baby was born. My mother was rocked on that hammock. I was rocked on that hammock, and when I brought my daughter as a baby to Abuela's house, she was held in Abuela's sun-browned arms, my porcelain pink baby, and rocked to a peaceful sleep too. She sits there and smiles as the breeze of a tropical November brings the scent of her roses and her herbs to us. She is proud of her garden. In front of the house she grows flowers and lush trailing plants; in the back, where the mango tree gives shade, she has an herb garden. From this patch of weedy-looking plants came all the remedies of my childhood, for anything from a sore throat to menstrual cramps. Abuela had a recipe for every pain that a child could dream up, and she brought it to your bed in her own hands smelling of the earth. For a moment I am content to sit in her comforting presence. She is rotund now; a small-boned brown-skinned earth mother—with a big heart and a temper to match. My grandfather comes to stand at the screen door. He has forgotten how the latch works. He pulls at the knob and moans softly, rattling it. With some effort Abuela gets down from the hammock. She opens the door, gently guiding the old man to a chair at the end of the porch. There he begins anew his constant search for the words he needs. He tries various combinations, but they don't work as language. Abuela pats his hand and motions for me to follow her into the house. We sit down at opposite ends of her sofa.

She apologizes to me as if for a misbehaving child.

"He'll quiet down," she says. "He does not like to be ignored."

I take a deep breath in preparation for my big lecture to Grandmother. This is the time to tell her that she has to give up trying to run this house and take care of others at her age. One of her daughters is prepared to take her in. Grandfather is to be sent to a nursing home. Before I can say anything, Abuela says: "Mi amor, would you like to hear a story?"

I smile, surprised at her offer. These are the same words that stopped me in my tracks as a child, even in the middle of a tantrum. Abuela could always entrance me with one of her tales. I nod. Yes, my sermon can wait a little longer, I thought.

"Let me tell you an old, old story I heard when I was a little girl.

"There was once a man who became worried and suspicious when he noticed that his wife disappeared from their bed every night for long periods of time. Wanting to find out what she was doing before confronting her, the man decided to stay awake at night and keep guard. For hours he watched her every movement through half-closed eyelids with his ears perked up like those of a burro.

"Then just about midnight, when the night was as dark as the bottom of a cauldron, he felt his wife slipping out of bed. He saw her go to the wardrobe and take out a jar and a little paintbrush. She stood naked by the window, and when the church bells struck twelve, she began to paint her entire body with the paintbrush, dipping it into the jar. As the bells tolled the hour, she whispered these words: *I don't believe in the church, or in God, or in the Virgin Mary.* As soon as this was spoken, she rose from the ground and flew into the night like a bird.

"Astounded, the man decided not to say anything to his wife the next day, but to try to find out where she went. The following night, the man pretended to sleep and waited until she had again performed her little ceremony and flown away, then he repeated her actions exactly. He soon found himself flying after her. Approaching a palace, he saw many other women circling the roof, taking turns going down the chimney. After the last had descended, he slid down the dark hole that led to the castle's bodega, where food and wine were stored. He hid himself behind some casks of wine and watched the women greet each other.

"The witches, for that's what they were, were the wives of his neighbors and friends, but he at first had trouble recognizing them, for like his wife, they were all naked. With much merriment, they took the meats and cheeses that hung from the bodega's rafters and laid a table for a feast. They drank the fine wines right from the bottles, like men in a cantina, and danced wildly to eerie music from invisible instruments. They spoke to each other in a language that he did not understand, words that sounded like a cat whose tail has been stepped on. Still, horrible as their speech was, the food they prepared smelled delicious. Cautiously placing himself in the shadows near one of the witches, he extended his hand for a plate. He was given a steaming dish of stewed tongue. Hungrily, he took a bite: it was tasteless. The other witches had apparently noticed the same thing, because they sent one of the younger ones to find some salt. But when the young witch came back into the room with a saltshaker in her hand, the man forgot himself and exclaimed: 'Thank God the salt is here.'

"On hearing God's name, all the witches took flight immediately, leaving the man completely alone in the darkened cellar. He tried the spell for flight that had brought him there, but it did not work. It was no longer midnight, and it was obviously the wrong incantation for going *up* a chimney. He tried all night to get out of the place, which had been left in shambles by the witches, but it was locked up as tight as heaven is to a sinner. Finally, he fell asleep from exhaustion, and slept until dawn, when he heard footsteps approaching. When he saw the heavy door being pushed open, he hid himself behind a cask of wine.

"A man in rich clothes walked in, followed by several servants. They were all armed with heavy sticks as if out to kill someone. When the man lit his torch and saw the chaos in the cellar, broken bottles strewn on the floor, meats and cheeses half-eaten and tossed everywhere, he cried out in such a rage that the man hiding behind the wine cask closed his eyes and committed his soul to God. The owner of the castle ordered his servants to search the whole bodega, every inch of it, until they discovered how vandals had entered his home. It was a matter of minutes before they discovered the witch's husband, curled up like a stray dog and, worse, painted the color of a vampire bat, without a stitch of clothing.

"They dragged him to the center of the room and beat him with their sticks until the poor man thought that his bones had been pulverized and he would have to be poured into his grave. When the castle's owner said that he thought the wretch had learned his lesson, the servants tossed him naked onto the road. The man was so sore that he slept right there on the public *camino*, oblivious to the stares and insults of all who passed him. When he awakened in the middle of the night and found himself naked, dirty, bloody, and miles from his home, he swore to himself right then and there that he would never, for anything in the world, follow his wife on her nightly journeys again."

"Colorín, colorado," Abuela claps her hands three times, chanting the childhood rhyme for ending a story, "Este cuento se ha acabado."

She smiles at me, shifting her position on the sofa to be able to watch Grandfather muttering to himself on the porch. I remember those eyes on me when I was a small child. Their movements seemed to be triggered by a child's actions, like those holograms of the Holy Mother that were popular with Catholics a few years ago— you couldn't get away from their mesmerizing gaze.

"Will you tell me about your year in New York, Abuela?" I surprise myself with the question. But suddenly I need to know about Abuela's lost year. It has to be another good story.

She looks intently at me before she answers. Her eyes are my eyes, same dark brown color, almond shape, and the lids that droop a little: called by some "bedroom eyes"; to others they are a sign of a cunning nature. "Why are you looking at me that way?" is a question I am often asked.

"I wanted to leave home," she says calmly, as though she had been expecting the question from me all along.

"You mean abandon your family?" I am really taken aback by her words.

"Yes, Hija. That is exactly what I mean. Abandon them. Never to return."

"Why?"

"I was tired. I was young and pretty, full of energy and dreams." She smiles as Grandfather breaks into song standing by himself on the porch. A woman passing by with a baby in her arms waves at him. Grandfather sings louder, something about a man going to his exile because the woman he loves has rejected him. He finishes the song on a long note and continues to stand in the middle of the tiled porch as if listening for applause. He bows.

Abuela shakes her head, smiling a little, as if amused by his antics, then she finishes her sentence, "Restless, bored. Four children and a husband all demanding more and more from me."

"So you left the children with your sister and went to New York?" I say, trying to keep the mixed emotions I feel out of my voice. I look at the serene old woman in front of me and cannot believe that she

47

once left four children and a loving husband to go live alone in a faraway country.

"I had left him once before, but he found me. I came back home, but on the condition that he never follow me anywhere again. I told him the next time I would not return." She is silent, apparently falling deep into thought.

"You were never really sick," I say, though I am afraid that she will not resume her story. But I want to know more about this woman whose life I thought was an open book.

"I *was* sick. Sick at heart. And he knew it," she says, keeping her eyes on Grandfather, who is standing as still as a marble statue on the porch. He seems to be listening intently for something.

"The year in New York was his idea. He saw how unhappy I was. He knew I needed to taste freedom. He paid my sister Delia to come take care of the children. He also sublet her apartment for me, though he had to take a second job to do it. He gave me money and told me to go."

"What did you do that year in New York?" I am both stunned and fascinated by Abuela's revelation. "I worked as a seamstress in a fancy dress shop. And . . . y pues, Hija," she smiles at me as if I should know some things without being told, "I lived."

"Why did you come back?" I ask.

"Because I love him," she says, "and I missed my children."

He is scratching at the door. Like a small child he has traced the sound of Abuela's voice back to her. She lets him in, guiding him gently by the hand. Then she eases him down on his favorite rocking chair. He begins to nod; soon he will be sound asleep, comforted by her proximity, secure in his familiar surroundings. I wonder how long it will take him to revert to infantilism. The doctors say he is physically healthy and may live for many years, but his memory, verbal skills, and ability to control his biological functions will deteriorate rapidly. He may end his days bedridden, perhaps comatose. My eyes fill with tears as I look at the lined face of this beautiful and gentle old man. I am in awe of the generosity of spirit that allowed him to give a year of freedom to the woman he loved, not knowing whether she would ever return to him. Abuela has seen my tears and moves over on the sofa to sit near me. She slips an arm around my waist and pulls me close. She kisses my wet cheek. Then she whispers softly into my ear, "and in time, the husband either began forgetting that he had seen her turn into a witch or believed that he had just dreamed it."

She takes my face into her hands. "I am going to take care of your grandfather until one of us dies. I promised him when I came back that I would never leave home again unless he asked me to: he never did. He never asked any questions."

I hear my mother's car pull up into the driveway. She will wait there for me. I will have to admit that I failed in my mission. I will argue Abuela's case without revealing her secret. As far as everyone is concerned she went away to recover from problems with her heart. That part is true in both versions of the story.

At the door she gives me the traditional blessing, adding with a wink, "Colorín, colorado." My grandfather, hearing her voice, smiles in his sleep.

Nada

Almost as soon as Doña Ernestina got the telegram about her son's having been killed in Vietnam, she started giving her possessions away. At first we didn't realize what she was doing. By the time we did, it was too late.

The army people had comforted Doña Ernestina with the news that her son's "remains" would have to be "collected and shipped" back to New Jersey at some later date, since other "personnel" had also been lost on the same day. In other words, she would have to wait until Tony's body could be processed.

Processed. Doña Ernestina spoke that word like a curse when she told us. We were all down in El Basement—that's what we called the cellar of our apartment building: no windows for light, boilers making such a racket that you could scream and almost no one would hear you. Some of us had started meeting here on Saturday mornings—as much to talk as to wash our clothes—and over the years it became a sort of women's club where we could catch up on a week's worth of gossip. That Saturday, however, I had dreaded going down the cement steps. All of us had just heard the news about Tony the night before.

I should have known the minute I saw her, holding court in her widow's costume, that something had cracked inside Doña Ernestina. She was in full luto—black from head to toe, including a mantilla. In contrast, Lydia and Isabelita were both in rollers and bathrobes: our customary uniform for these Saturday morning gatherings—maybe our way of saying "No Men Allowed." As I approached them, Lydia stared at me with a scared-rabbit look in her eyes.

Doña Ernestina simply waited for me to join the other two leaning against the machines before she continued explaining what had happened when the news of Tony had arrived at her door the day before.

She spoke calmly, a haughty expression on her face, looking like an offended duchess in her beautiful black dress. She was pale, pale, but she had a wild look in her eyes. The officer had told her that—when the time came—they would bury Tony with "full military honors"; for now they were sending her the medal and a flag. But she had said, "No, *gracias*," to the funeral, and she sent the flag and medals back marked *Ya no vive aquí*: Does not live here anymore. "Tell the Mr. President of the United States what I say: No, gracias."

Then she waited for our response.

Lydia shook her head, indicating that she was speechless. And Elenita looked pointedly at me, forcing me to be the one to speak the words of sympathy for all of us, to reassure Doña Ernestina that she had done exactly what any of us would have done in her place: yes, we would have all said *No, gracias*, to any president who had actually tried to pay for a son's life with a few trinkets and a folded flag.

Doña Ernestina nodded gravely. Then she picked up the stack of neatly folded men's shirts from the sofa (a discard we had salvaged from the sidewalk) and walked regally out of El Basement.

Lydia, who had gone to high school with Tony, burst into tears as soon as Doña Ernestina was out of sight. Elenita and I sat her down between us on the sofa and held her until she had let most of it out. Lydia is still young—a woman who has not yet been visited too often by *la muerte*. Her husband of six months has just gotten his draft notice, and they have been trying for a baby—trying very hard. The walls of El Building are thin enough so that it has become a secret joke (kept only from Lydia and Roberto) that he is far more likely to escape the draft due to acute exhaustion than by becoming a father.

"Doesn't Doña Ernestina feel *anything?*" Lydia asked in between sobs. "Did you see her, dressed up like an actress in a play—and not one tear for her son?"

"We all have different ways of grieving," I said, though I couldn't help thinking that there *was* a strangeness to Doña Ernestina and that Lydia was right when she said that the woman seemed to be acting out a part. "I think we should wait and see what she is going to do."

"Maybe," said Elenita. "Did you get a visit from *el padre* yester-day?"

We nodded, not surprised to learn that all of us had gotten personal calls from Padre Álvaro, our painfully shy priest, after Doña Ernestina had frightened him away. Apparently el padre had come to her apartment immediately after hearing about Tony, expecting to comfort the woman as he had when Don Antonio died suddenly a year ago. Her grief then had been understandable in its immensity, for she had been burying not only her husband but also the dream shared by many of the barrio women her age—that of returning with her man to the Island after retirement, of buying a *casita* in the old pueblo, and of being buried on native ground alongside *la familia*. People *my* age—those of us born or raised here—have had our mothers drill this fantasy into our brains all of our lives. So when Don Antonio dropped his head on the domino table, scattering the ivory pieces of the best game of the year, and when he was laid out in his best black suit at Ramírez's Funeral Home, all of us knew how to talk to the grieving widow.

That was the last time we saw both her men. Tony was there, too—home on a two-day pass from basic training—and he cried like a little boy over his father's handsome face, calling him Papi, Papi. Doña Ernestina had had a full mother's duty then, taking care of the hysterical boy. It was a normal chain of grief, the strongest taking care of the weakest. We buried Don Antonio at Garden State Memorial Park, where there are probably more Puerto Ricans than on the Island. Padre Álvaro said his sermon in a soft, trembling voice that was barely audible over the cries of the boy being supported on one side by his mother, impressive in her quiet strength and dignity, and on the other by Cheo, owner of the bodega where Don Antonio had played dominoes with other barrio men of his age for over twenty years.

Just about everyone from El Building had attended that funeral, and it had been done right. Doña Ernestina had sent her son off to fight for America and then had started collecting her widow's pension. Some of us asked Doña Iris (who knew how to read cards) about Doña Ernestina's future, and Doña Iris had said: "A long journey within a year"—which fit with what we had thought would happen next: Doña Ernestina would move back to the Island and wait with her relatives for Tony to come home from the war. Some older women actually went home when they started collecting social security or pensions, but that was rare. Usually, it seemed to me, somebody had to die before the island dream would come true for women like Doña Ernestina. As for my friends and me, we talked about "vacations" in the Caribbean. But we knew that if life was hard for us in this barrio, it would be worse in a pueblo where no one knew us (and had maybe only heard of our parents before they came to *Los Estados Unidos de América*, where most of us had been brought as children).

When Padre Álvaro had knocked softly on my door, I had yanked it open, thinking it was that ex-husband of mine asking for a second chance again. (That's just the way Miguel knocks when he's sorry for leaving me—about once a week—when he wants a loan.) So I was wearing my go-to-hell face when I threw open the door, and the poor priest nearly jumped out of his skin. I saw him take a couple of deep breaths before he asked me in his slow way—he tries to hide his stutter by dragging out his words—if I knew whether or not Doña Ernestina was ill. After I said, "No, not that I know," Padre Álvaro just stood there, looking pitiful, until I asked him if he cared to come in. I had been sleeping on the sofa and watching TV all afternoon, and I really didn't want him to see the mess, but I had nothing to fear. The poor man actually took one step back at my invitation. No, he was in a hurry, he had a few other parishioners to visit, etc. These were difficult times, he said, so-so-so many young people lost to drugs or dying in the wa-wa-war. I asked him if *he* thought Doña Ernestina was sick, but he just shook his head. The man looked like an orphan at my door with those sad, brown eyes. He was actually appealing in a homely way: that long nose nearly touched the tip of his chin when he smiled, and his big crooked teeth broke my heart.

"She does not want to speak to me," Padre Álvaro said as he caressed a large silver crucifix that hung on a thick chain around his neck. He seemed to be dragged down by its weight, stoop-shouldered and skinny as he was.

I felt a strong impulse to feed him some of my chicken soup, still warm on the stove from my supper. Contrary to what Lydia says about me behind my back, I like living by myself. And I could not have been happier to have that mama's boy Miguel back where he belonged—with his mother, who thought that he was still her baby. But this scraggly thing at my door needed home cooking and maybe even something more than a hot meal to bring a little spark into his life. (I mentally asked God to forgive me for having thoughts like these about one of his priests. *Ay bendito*, but they too are made of flesh and blood.)

"Maybe she just needs a little more time, Padre," I said in as comforting a voice as I could manage. Unlike the other women in El Building, I am not convinced that priests are truly necessary—or even much help—in times of crisis.

"Sí, Hija, perhaps you're right," he muttered sadly—calling me "daughter" even though I'm pretty sure I'm five or six years older. (Padre Álvaro seems so "untouched" that it's hard to tell his age. I mean, when you live, it shows. He looks hungry for love, starving himself by choice.) I promised him that I would look in on Doña Ernestina. Without another word, he made the sign of the cross in the air between us and turned away. As I heard his slow steps descending the creaky stairs, I asked myself: what do priests dream about?

When el padre's name came up again during that Saturday meeting in El Basement, I asked my friends what *they* thought a priest dreamed about. It was a fertile subject, so much so that we spent the rest of our laundry time coming up with scenarios. Before the last dryer stopped, we all agreed that we could not receive communion the next day at mass unless we went to confession that afternoon and told another priest, not Álvaro, about our "unclean thoughts."

As for Doña Ernestina's situation, we agreed that we should be there for her if she called, but the decent thing to do, we decided, was give her a little more time alone. Lydia kept repeating, in that childish way of hers, "Something is wrong with the woman," but she didn't volunteer to go see what it was that was making Doña Ernestina act so strangely. Instead she complained that she and Roberto had heard pots and pans banging and things being moved around for hours in 4-D last night—they had hardly been able to sleep. Isabelita winked at me behind Lydia's back. Lydia and Roberto still had not caught on: if they could hear what was going on in 4-D, the rest of us could also get an earful of what went on in 4-A. They were just kids who thought they had invented sex: I tell you, a telenovela could be made from the stories in El Building.

On Sunday Doña Ernestina was not at the Spanish mass and I avoided Padre Álvaro so he would not ask me about her. But I was worried. Doña Ernestina was a church cucaracha—a devout Catholic who, like many of us, did not always do what the priests and the Pope ordered but who knew where God lived. Only a serious illness or tragedy could keep her from attending mass, so afterward I went straight to her apartment and knocked on her door. There was no answer, although I had heard scraping and dragging noises, like furniture being moved around. At least she was on her feet and active. Maybe housework was what she needed to snap out of her shock. I decided to try again the next day.

As I went by Lydia's apartment, the young woman opened her door—I knew she had been watching me through the peephole—to tell me about more noises from across the hall during the night. Lydia was in her baby-doll pajamas. Although she stuck only her nose out, I could see Roberto in his jockey underwear doing something in the kitchen. I couldn't help thinking about Miguel and me when we had first gotten together. We were an explosive combination. After a night of passionate lovemaking, I would walk around thinking: Do not light cigarettes around me. No open flames. Highly combustible materials being transported. But when his mama showed up at our door, the man of fire turned into a heap of ashes at her feet.

"Let's wait and see what happens," I told Lydia again.

We did not have to wait for long. On Monday Doña Ernestina called to invite us to a wake for Tony, a *velorio*, in her apartment. The word spread fast. Everyone wanted to do something for her. Cheo donated fresh chickens and island produce of all kinds. Several of us got together and made arroz con pollo, also flan for dessert. And Doña Iris made two dozen *pasteles* and wrapped the meat pies in banana leaves that she had been saving in her freezer for her famous Christmas parties. We women carried in our steaming plates, while the men brought in their bottles of Palo Viejo rum for themselves and candy-sweet Manischewitz wine for us. We came ready to spend the night saying our rosaries and praying for Tony's soul.

Doña Ernestina met us at the door and led us into her living room, where the lights were off. A photograph of Tony and one of her deceased husband Don Antonio were sitting on top of a table, surrounded by at least a dozen candles. It was a spooky sight that caused several of the older women to cross themselves. Doña Ernestina had arranged folding chairs in front of this table and told us to sit down. She did not ask us to take our food and drinks to the kitchen. She just looked at each of us individually, as if she were taking attendance in a class, and then said: "I have asked you here to say good-bye to my husband Antonio and my son Tony. You have been my friends and neighbors for twenty years, but they were my life. Now that they are gone, I have nada. Nada. Nada."

I tell you, that word is like a drain that sucks everything down. Hearing her say *nada* over and over made me feel as if I were being yanked into a dark pit. I could feel the others getting nervous around me too, but here was a woman deep into her pain: we had to give her a little space. She looked around the room, then walked out without saying another word.

As we sat there in silence, stealing looks at each other, we began to hear the sounds of things being moved around in other rooms. One of the older women took charge then, and soon the drinks were poured, the food served—all this while the strange sounds kept coming from different rooms in the apartment. Nobody said much, except once when we heard something like a dish fall and break. Doña Iris pointed her index finger at her ear and made a couple of circles—and out of nervousness, I guess, some of us giggled like schoolchildren.

It was a long while before Doña Ernestina came back out to us. By then we were gathering our dishes and purses, having come to the conclusion that it was time to leave. Holding two huge Sears shopping bags, one in each hand, Doña Ernestina took her place at the front door as if she were a society hostess in a receiving line. Some of us women hung back to see what was going on. But Tito, the building's super, had had enough and tried to get past her. She took his hand, putting in it a small ceramic poodle with a gold chain around its neck. Tito gave the poodle a funny look, then glanced at Doña Ernestina as though he were scared and hurried away with the dog in his hand.

We were let out of her place one by one but not until she had forced one of her possessions on each of us. She grabbed without looking from her bags. Out came her prized *miniaturas*, knickknacks that take a woman a lifetime to collect. Out came ceramic and porcelain items of all kinds, including vases and ashtrays; out came kitchen utensils, dishes, forks, knives, spoons; out came old calendars and every small item that she had touched or been touched by in the last twenty years. Out came a bronzed baby shoe—and I got that.

As we left the apartment, Doña Iris said "Psst" to some of us, so we followed her down the hallway. "Doña Ernestina's faculties are temporarily out of order," she said very seriously. "It is due to the shock of her son's death."

We all said "Sí" and nodded our heads.

"But what can we do?" Lydia said, her voice cracking a little. "What should I do with this?" She was holding one of Tony's baseball trophies in her hand: 1968 Most Valuable Player, for the Pocos Locos, our barrio's team.

Doña Iris said, "Let us keep her things safe for her until she recovers her senses. And let her mourn in peace. These things take time. If she needs us, she will call us." Doña Iris shrugged her shoulders. "*Así es la vida, hijas:* that's the way life is."

As I passed Tito on the stairs, he shook his head while looking up at Doña Ernestina's door: "I say she needs a shrink. I think somebody should call the social worker." He did not look at me when he mumbled these things. By "somebody" he meant one of us women. He didn't want trouble in his building, and he expected one of us to get rid of the problems. I just ignored him.

In my bed I prayed to the Holy Mother that she would find peace for Doña Ernestina's troubled spirit, but things got worse. All that week Lydia saw strange things happening through the peephole on her door. Every time people came to Doña Ernestina's apartment— to deliver flowers, or telegrams from the Island, or anything—the woman would force something on them. She pleaded with them to take this or that; if they hesitated, she commanded them with those tragic eyes to accept a token of her life.

And they did, walking out of our apartment building, carrying cushions, lamps, doilies, clothing, shoes, umbrellas, wastebaskets, schoolbooks, and notebooks: things of value and things of no worth at all to anyone but the person who had owned them. Eventually winos and street people got the news of the great giveaway in 4-D, and soon there was a line down the stairs and out the door. Nobody went home empty-handed; it was like a soup kitchen. Lydia was afraid to step out of her place because of all the dangerous-looking characters hanging out on that floor. And the smell! Entering our building was like coming into a cheap bar and public urinal combined.

Isabelita, living alone with her two little children and fearing for their safety, was the one who finally called a meeting of the residents. Only the women attended, since the men were truly afraid of Doña Ernestina. It isn't unusual for men to be frightened when they see a woman go crazy. If they are not the cause of her madness, then they act as if they don't understand it and usually leave us alone to deal with our "woman's problems." This is just as well.

Maybe I *am* just bitter because of Miguel—I know what is said behind my back. But this is a fact: when a woman is in trouble, a man calls in her mama, her sisters, or her friends, and then he makes himself scarce until it's all over. This happens again and again. At how many bedsides of women have I sat? How many times have I made the doctor's appointment, taken care of the children, and fed the husbands of my friends in the barrio? It is not that the men can't do these things; it's just that they know how much women help each other. Maybe the men even suspect that we know one another better than they know their own wives. As I said, it is just as well that they stay out of our way when there is trouble. It makes things simpler for us.

At the meeting, Isabelita said right away that we should go up to 4-D and try to reason with *la pobre* Doña Ernestina. Maybe we could get her to give us a relative's address in Puerto Rico—the woman obviously needed to be taken care of. What she was doing was putting us all in a very difficult situation. There were no dissenters this time. We voted to go as a group to talk to Doña Ernestina the next morning.

But that night we were all awakened by crashing noises on the street. In the light of the full moon, I could see that the air was raining household goods: kitchen chairs, stools, a small TV, a nightstand, pieces of a bed frame. Everything was splintering as it landed on the pavement. People were running for cover and yelling up at our building. The problem, I knew instantly, was in apartment 4-D.

Putting on my bathrobe and slippers, I stepped out into the hallway. Lydia and Roberto were rushing down the stairs, but on the flight above my landing, I caught up with Doña Iris and Isabelita, heading toward 4-D. Out of breath, we stood in the fourth-floor hallway, listening to police sirens approaching our building in front. We could hear the slamming of car doors and yelling—in both Spanish and English. Then we tried the door to 4-D. It was unlocked.

We came into a room virtually empty. Even the pictures had been taken down from the walls; all that was left were the nail holes and the lighter places on the paint where the framed photographs had been for years. We took a few seconds to spot Doña Ernestina: she was curled up in the farthest corner of the living room, naked.

"Cómo salió a este mundo," said Doña Iris, crossing herself.

Just as she had come into the world. Wearing nothing. Nothing around her except a clean, empty room. Nada. She had left nothing behind—except the bottles of pills, the ones the doctors give to ease the pain, to numb you, to make you feel nothing when someone dies.

The bottles were empty too, and the policemen took them. But we didn't let them take Doña Ernestina until we each had brought up some of our own best clothes and dressed her like the decent woman that she was. *La decencia*. Nothing can ever change that—not even la muerte. This is the way life is. *Así es la vida*.

Letter from a Caribbean Island

June 25, 1990
Boquerón Beach
Puerto Rico

Dear Ellen,

Last night the old man who lived in the cabin next to mine found what he came for. As I told you in my last letter, he was here in Boquerón, trying to spot dolphins. At first I thought he was senile or crazy. But every night after the beach cleared of people, he would sit under the lamppost, sketching on a pad. In the mornings he sculpted in clay from his drawings. The figures he made are tiny—mostly sea creatures. He let them dry on the porch table. I watched him from my hammock while pretending to read.

Last night the sea was like a black mirror. I was feeling good for the first time since the baby. I had taken my *Ulysses* out to the porch and was enjoying the streets of Dublin through the eyes of that time traveler Leopold Bloom when I heard someone cry out—it was a shout of joy, not distress. I looked up and saw the old man running toward the water, arms waving, like a racer coming up on the finish line. He looked at once frail and wild as a young boy—without thinking, I ran out after him. It was then that I saw them too. Dolphins. Three or four of them; I couldn't be certain. I can't tell you why, but tears came to my eyes when I saw those calm faces with their undulating smiles break through the moon's reflection on the water.

The old man ignored my shouts about the undertow. I threw off my robe and jumped in after him, but he was faster than I had imagined. The last time I saw him he had his arms around one of the placid creatures, letting it carry him too far out to sea for me to follow. I called the police right away, and they searched all night and this morning. No trace. Sharks, not dolphins, they are speculating.

But I saw them in the moonlight, and I heard them sing. Ellen, I took one of his figures that was drying in the sun. It is a tiny siren sitting on a rock, waving. I will show it to you when I get home. I am finally beginning to believe that I will heal. In time.

Love,
Marina

Guard Duty

In my Spanish-language childhood
I was put under the care
of *El Ángel de la Guarda,*

my Guardian Angel, the military guard
who required a nightly salute, a plea
on my knees for protection
against the dangers hidden in dreams,
and from night-prowling demons.

In the print framed over my bed,
he was portrayed as a feathered androgyny
hovering above two barefoot children
whose features were set in pastel horror—

and no wonder—under the bridge
they were crossing yawned
a sulfurous abyss—their only light being
the glow of the thing with wings
otherwise invisible to them.

I could take no comfort in this dark
nursery myth, as some nights
I lay awake listening to the murmur
of my parents' voices

sharing their incomprehensible plans
in a well-lit kitchen, while I brooded
over the cruel indifference of adults
who abandoned children to the night,

and about that *Comandante* in the sky
who knew everything I did, or thought of doing,
whose soldier could so calmly smile
while innocent children crossed over darkness,
alone, afraid, night after night.

The Purpose of Nuns

As a young girl attending Sunday mass,
I'd watch them float down the nave
in their medieval somberness, the calm
of salvation on the pink oval of their faces
framed by tight-fitting coifs. They seemed above
the tedious cycle of confession, penance
and absolution they supervised: of weekday dreams
told to a stranger on Saturday; of Sunday sermons long
as a sickroom visit, and the paranoia of God always
watching you—that made me hide under my blanket
to read forbidden fictions.

Some of us were singled out for our plainness,
our inclination to solitude, or perhaps—
as our mothers hoped in their secret hearts—
our auras of spiritual light only these brides
of quietness could see in us. We were led to retreats,
where our uninitiated footsteps were softened,
and our heartbeats synchronized, becoming one
with the sisters'. In their midst, we sensed freedom
from the worry of flesh—the bodies of nuns
being merely spirit slips under their thick garments.
There was also the appeal of sanctuary in a spotless mansion
permeated with the smells of baked bread, polished wood
and leather-bound volumes of only good words.
And in the evenings, the choral mystery of vespers
in Latin, casting the final spell of community over us.

The purpose of nuns was to remind us
of monochrome peace in a world splashed in violent colors.

And sometimes, exhausted by the pounding demands
of adolescence, I'd let my soul alight
on the possibility of cloistered life, but once the sky
cleared, opening up like a blue highway to anywhere,
I'd resume my flight back to the world.

The Game

The little humpbacked girl
did not go to school,
but was kept home to help her mother,
an unsmiling woman with other children
whose spines were not twisted
into the symbol of a family's shame.

At birth,
on first seeing the child
curled into a question mark,
the eternal *why*
she would have to carry home,
she gave her the name of Cruz,
for the cross Christ bore
to Calvary.

In my house,
we did not speak of her affliction,
but acted as if Cruz,
whose lovely head
sat incongruously upon a body
made of stuck-together parts—
like a child's first attempt
at cutting and pasting a paper doll—
was the same
as any of my other friends.

But when she stood at our door,
waiting for me to go out and play,
Mother fell silent, awed, perhaps,
by the sight
of one of her God's small mysteries.

Running to her backyard,
Cruz and I would enter a playhouse
she had built of palm fronds
where we'd play her favorite game: "family."
I was always cast in the role
of husband or child—perfect
in my parts—I'd praise her lavishly
for the imaginary dishes
she placed before me,
while she laughed, delighted
at my inventions, lost in the game,
until it started getting too late
to play pretend.

The Lesson of the Teeth

I heard my mother say it once
in the kitchen—that to dream of teeth
means death is coming, rattling
its bag of bones as a warning to all
to say a "Credo" every night before sleeping.

One day, as a child, seeking the mystery
of my Aunt Clotilde's beauty,
I slipped into her bedroom without knocking.
She was sitting at her vanity,
combing her long black hair everyone said
I'd inherited. A set of false teeth
floated in a jar beside her. In horror,
I looked up into the face of a sunken-cheeked hag
in the mirror—then ran all the way home.

She must have seen me but never let on.
Her face filled with flesh appeared often
at our place. But her smile
sent a little current of icy fear up my spine—
that message they say you receive
when someone steps on your grave.

They Never Grew Old

I am speaking of that hollow-eyed race
of bone-embraced tubercular women and men,
the last of whom I caught a glimpse of
in the final days of my childhood.

Every family had one
hidden away in a sanitarium—
a word whispered when certain names
came up in conversation. And when I asked
my mother what it meant, she said
a very clean place.

Once, I saw one; a rare
appearance by a distant cousin
our family tried to keep invisible.
From a neighbor's house across the road,
I looked upon the visitor in a white dress
that seemed to hang upon her skeletal frame
like a starched garment on a wire hanger.
She held a handkerchief to her mouth
the entire time. The circle of polite relatives
sat back in the chairs around her.
The coffee cup at her side would later
be discarded, the chair she floated on—she seemed
to have no volume or weight—would be scrubbed
with something so strong it made one cry; the whole house
sanitized and disinfected after her brief stay.

Though these sad, thin cousins were rarely seen
in our living rooms, they were a presence in the attics
and closets where we kept all our unwanted kin.

And they too had their heroes and myths.

As a girl I heard the story of two young people,
put away to die and forgotten,
who met in the cool, pine-scented corridors
of their hospital prison and fell in love.
Desperate to be together, they escaped
into the night. It was a young woman
who found them under an embankment bridge,
a damp place where a creek one could step over ran.
Lying in each others' arms, their bodies were marbleized
with fever and morning dew. They were a frieze
in a Roman catacomb: Eros and Psyche in repose.

Moved by their plight, the girl brought them food
and a blanket. But dying creatures are easy to track,
and they were soon found by townspeople scandalized
that the ill should want to make love. A priest
was called in before a doctor. I surmise
that they died in separate beds.
                        Back then, I was convinced
the story of the dying lovers clinging to each other
in the dark cave was the most romantic thing I would ever hear.
The spot on their lungs that killed them I imagined
as a privileged place on the body's ordinary geography.

I too wanted to live in *a very clean place,*
where fragile as a pale pink rosebud I would sit
among my many satin pillows and wait for the man with whom
I would never grow old, to rescue me from a dull life.
Death and love once again confused
by one too young to see the difference.

Nothing Wasted

Mother always kept
something growing in our homes. Every navy order
to move made her worry
about the seeds she'd started in rented yards.
But there was always one on her kitchen counter
she could take with her—a jar of murky water
containing an avocado pit
pierced through with a toothpick, looking like
a preserved Sacred Heart.
                                        Last summer
I stayed in her room in an old house
in Puerto Rico, where she has dug herself in,
in the middle of a chaotic garden
that encroaches on windows and doors
like the end of civilization.
                                        On her bedroom window
hung a cage with three doves; a female
and two wary males. The peace of the nest
had recently been disturbed
by the egg she sat on, ensconced
on a coconut shell half,
hanging from wires. Her mates kept watch
from perches across the cage, jealous
of her attention.
                                        I'd fallen asleep
to their cooing, then jumped up startled
by the frantic beat of wings against metal,
and the unmistakable finality
of the egg breaking.

                              I did not rise
to face the loss—but watched her tiptoe in,
reach to scoop up the pieces, then toss it
out the window into the thick vegetation
that would absorb it as nourishment.

Then she whispered, *sleep well,*
comforting me with her voice,
like all the nights she tucked me into new beds,
telling me about the new garden she would start
as soon as the last box was unpacked,
talking away my fear of the dark
one more time.

Women Who Love Angels

They are thin
and rarely marry, living out
their long lives
in spacious rooms, French doors
giving view to formal gardens
where aromatic flowers
grow in profusion.
They play their pianos
in the late afternoon
tilting their heads
at a gracious angle
as if listening
to notes pitched above
the human range.
Age makes them translucent;
each palpitation of their hearts
visible at temple or neck.
When they die, it's in their sleep,
their spirits shaking gently loose
from a hostess too well bred
to protest.

To Grandfather, Now Forgetting

He was a master carpenter and musician
who used the rhythms of hammer and brush
to make poems and songs as he worked.

He was dark and intense,
prone to melancholy;
a handsome man
who wore his hat at the back of his head.
Weekends, he traveled the island
playing the guitar and singing
his own songs at coming-of-age parties,
where the girls
were flowers in a formal garden
he was privileged to walk through.

The mango fruit, he once said to me,
with its juice that drowns you
in sweetness, should be eaten
with closed eyes.

As a boy he had left home
to apprentice with an old man
who taught him how to find the grain of wood;
about the secret lives of pigments,
and in the fading light of the day,
how to make music with roughened hands.

The day he first saw her,
he was filled with music. The words
to the song he'd write for her that night
came to him like grace after a prayer.
And he followed the proud girl
into her fifteenth year
with the fascination of a sleepwalker
pulled from his bed by moonbeams.

She was a tamarind tree in full bloom,
her brown skin naturally perfumed
like a flower opening in the night.
When she moved—her body became a bolero,
a seduction with violins. Looking at her
he heard his own voice echoing
deep in the hollow of his chest,
starting a sweet ache. And he became aware
of his loneliness.

But she turned away from his suppliant's eyes,
and danced with others in the crowded room
where he was making music
for her alone. She made him play hard
for her love, knowing life with a poet
would not be easy.

The year I came back to his house,
at fifteen, I wore my Indian dress
sewn through with tiny mirrors.
I stood before my grandfather
while he walked around me as if I were
a winding corridor at Versailles, caught
by the sight of his many selves
reflected on me. He said: *Niña*,

I see you have learned that the way
to conquer is to divide.

Papá,
tonight I want to wear that dress for you,
lift you out of that shroud of silence,
and take you to a fiesta,
where we can dance until the woman you will love
catches your eye, and you can recall
the words to your song,
and everything can start again.

My Grandfather's Hat

In memory of Basiliso Morot Cordero

I cannot stop thinking of that old hat
he is wearing in the grave: the last gift
of love from his wife before they fell
into the habit of silence.

Forgotten as the daughters chose
the funeral clothes, it sat
on his dresser as it always had:
old leather, aromatic of his individual self,
pliable as an old companion, ready to go
anywhere with him.

The youngest grandchild remembered
and ran after her father, who was carrying
the old man's vanilla suit—the one worn to *bodas*,
bautismos, and elections—like a lifeless
child in his arms: *No te olvides
del sombrero de abuelo.*

I had seen him hold the old hat in his lap
and caress it as he talked of the good times
and, when he walked outside, place it on his head
like a blessing.

My grandfather, who believed in God,
the Gracious Host, Proprietor of the Largest Hacienda.
May it be so. May heaven
be an island in the sun,
where a good man may wear his hat with pride,
glad that he could take it with him.

78

Blood

They poured it into his veins
until he became someone else, a drunken man as he tries
to rise from the hospital bed, where the stained sheets
are a testament of shame to the anonymous nights
spent with the stranger his body has become.

He slides down feet first
like a child, hoping his legs will not betray him.
But he gets dizzy looking down at the reflective tiles.

Hanging onto the rails,
he sees himself flat on the ground, until the nurse
leads him by the elbow into the sunlight.
Outside, he is hurt by a world where every surface
is a mirror of steel or plastic.

No place
for an old man avoiding his own face like a good friend
he has offended.

The Life of an Echo

Until Manuel,
I preferred the company of shadows
to the vagrant love of men.
                  One day,
he came to my door to slake his thirst,
impatient to be on his way
to anyplace.
            I was drawn
to his quick speech,
the little red flag of his tongue
signaling his body's intentions.

I began to understand how the wind
can make you feel naked.
When he took my face in his hands,

I was chaos on the first day,
waiting for the Word.
                Yet after
we answered the call of the flesh, nothing
remained but the valley's deep emptiness,
returning my voice.

Juana: An Old Story

Though her home is deep in the country,
Juana can hear the bells of vespers clearly.
She has not set foot in church since she lost
the child. She prays alone. Three months

without a word from Carlos, and the last letter
held no future for them with its chatter of snow
falling like coconut shavings from the sky, its joke
that it was Mary making holiday treats
for the saints. Juana crosses herself for the blasphemy.

Her days have been an endless progression
of heartbeats; nights, a slow-moving river she floats on,
pain like a small animal digging into the muddy bottom
of the past. On her knees by the window

facing the town sinking into darkness, rooftops
and church spires held aloft in orange clouds
that are God's fiery hands, she breathes in
the warm, vegetative air. Evenings,
coming in from the fields, her man had once brought her
the aroma of growing things—coffee beans, sugarcane—

on his skin. Juana counts Hail Marys on her rosary,
giving each red bead the name of a child: Rosita,
Ramón, Jazmínes, José.

The Campesino's Lament

It is Ash Wednesday, and Christ is waiting
to die. I have left my fields dark and moist
from last night's rain, to take the sacrament.
My face is streaked with ashes. Come back,
Mujer. Without you,
                            I am an empty place
where spiders crawl and nothing takes root.
Today, taking the Host, I remembered
your hands—incense and earth, fingertips
like white grapes I would take into my mouth
one by one.
                    When I enter the house,
it resists me like an angry woman. Our room,
your things, the bed—a penance
I offer up for Lent. Waking with you,
I would fill myself with the morning,
in sweet mango breaths. Watching you sleep,
I willed my dreams into you.

But clouds cannot be harvested, nor children
wished into life.

                    In the wind that may travel
as far as you have gone, I send this message: Out here,
in a place you will not forget, a simple man
has been moved to curse the rising sun and to question
God's unfinished work.

Las Magdalenas

While it's still dark,
they drape shawls over their sequins,
swing black-stockinged legs
out of long cars parked a block
or two away. The five A.M. mass
is preferred, convenient.
              On entering the dim nave
they begin to shed *la vida:* stale
perfume absorbed by the censer
the angelic altar boy swings
as he leads the sleepy man
in scarlet robes—no less splendid
than the women's evening clothes—
to the altar—the man with the soft hands
who does not touch women, the one
who can drive the money changers away
from the temples of their bodies.
              Each Sunday it is the same,
like sweeping sand from a house on the beach.
They bow their heads to accept
what was promised Magdalene.
The tired man serves them humbly
at his master's table. He breaks the bread
and pours the inexhaustible wine.

"Peace be with you." He sends them away
an hour before dawn. "And with you,"
they reply in unison, yawning
into their mantillas, ready now
for the clean sheets of their absolution.

Olga

After a double-shift day at the denim factory,
Olga comes into the bodega for a bottle
of sweet red wine and a pack of Salems.
She smells like new blue jeans. Sighing
her exhaustion, she leans on the counter
while Mario gives her change,
lining up quarters, nickels, and dimes
in a silver road to her palm.

Olga laughs and starts to sing
an old Island song in a voice of *melao,*
sugarcane syrup: *canción muy dulce
y dolorosa.* She hums hot sun balm
into her tired limbs, conjures an ocean wind
that lifts her to her feet,
and hibiscus blossoms rise in a blush
to her cheeks.

Mario plays soft, seductive bongos
on the formica, watches her moving away,
hips keeping time to his beat.

Out on the street,
Olga braces against the chill. Cradling the bottle
between her breasts, she hurries home
just a few steps before night falls.

Dear Joaquín

This may never reach your hands. It is unlikely that it will. With your mamá watching her nest like a jealous hen and Rosaura keeping you drugged with sex and her witch's brews. You are lucky if you still know your name, much less remember me, the woman who truly loves you. Joaquín, I wait for you in America. My love, I come home from the factory every day to an empty, cold room. I am drinking a glass of our favorite wine—you once said my skin tasted like this— and writing to you, sealing all my hopes in this envelope. This is unbearable, mi amor. How could you abandon me when I needed you the most? Do you know that after my mother caught us on the beach that night she locked me in my room and called the priest in to confess me? I felt like a murderer on death row. I told him I was almost eighteen, a woman now, older than my mother when she had me. He refused me absolution and walked out of our house. Mamá came in yelling, *mala, perdida,* and said I was no longer her daughter. On my birthday that Sunday, Joaquín, I got two gifts from my family: a suitcase and a one-way ticket to New York City. But you must have heard all this. At first I thought you would come to me, but ten months have passed and not a word. My sister finally wrote me that you were hiding in your mother's house, from my mother's fury and the priest's tongue, and about Rosaura. You, hiding like a frightened child. You, my brave Joaquín of the night, my valiant Joaquín of the moon, the sand, skin, and wine. Hiding behind your mamá's big bottom, under Rosaura's mambo skirts. I will write to you every day of this long winter. My letters will gather like a storm cloud over your clear blue island sky until they burst in a downpour. The passion that you awakened in me will shadow you, Joaquín, until I come home to claim you. You are my man. In the meantime, forget about Rosaura. That *bruja* has put you under a spell. Don't eat any-

85

thing from her *cocina*. And keep my image in your mind, Joaquín. If this page should find its way to you, write to me and tell me how it is on the *playa* now. Tell me how it is to feel the sun on your skin in November.

Amor y besos
Olga

Lydia

I haven't seen her in twenty years—then she swoops down among the relatives in black for my father's funeral. Lydia tells me she has found God in New York City. I see that she wears no makeup, her skirt covers her knees. She holds a Bible like a small black purse on her lap. My last image of her is a bird's-eye view from my bedroom window of her emerging out of a breath-steamed red Mustang that spewed her on the street like a crumpled sack in her tan coat, then cut a wheel into the night. I let her in from the forbidden date, lied to her mother on the telephone—*Tía, we lost track of time, can Lydia spend the night?* I take the risk of punishment myself, banished from my pious aunt's house, for the secondhand thrill Lydia had promised, the account of her despoilment. Time has made her substantial. She fulfills her blouse, strains the darts, and puts pressure on the seams. And she carries the weight of revelation like an ark on her wide shoulders. Although I search her face for a trace of the old humor, trying to lock our eyes in old conspiracies, her pupils are hard and smooth as the pebbles she used to carry in her purse to signal her homecomings from sin by throwing them at my window. As payment she'd bring me a venial harvest in the smoke smell of her hair, a hotel ashtray, matches advertising easy money schemes, and once—a man's handkerchief with the initials of someone I could never look again in the eye at family reunions. Lydia's winks across our living rooms were a coded key to secrets we shared. *He is everywhere,* she says now, and I half expect her to produce proof out of her large handbag; *tangibles,* as I called the artifacts she brought me from her forays. Instead she digs out a small book of psalms and sets it down between us on the sofa. She takes her leave with a quick hug and a blessing and rushes out of my house, giving me what she still believes is all I need: a token of her experience.

Vida

My lover is the old poet Gabriel,
who lives on a mountain,
high above the rest of us—in the place, he says,
where sadness makes its nest.

Day begins with the first cry of a child,
Gabriel writes his laments for an age,
then he is stolen by a stranger dressed in black.
                              On nights
when the moon lights the way,
I climb the rocky hill to his home.
He is always at the window, waiting for me,
or for daybreak; I do not ask.

When I hold this old man in my arms,
his thin body light as bird bones, I feel
as if I were warming a wounded sparrow.
His gray eyes are darkening. He is writing words
for the stone carver.
                      By autumn,
I will be gathering flowers for his grave:
a basketful of bird-of-paradise,
the ones he called in a poem a flock
of yellow-crested cockateels. I will pick
flame-of-the-forest, the fire orange blossom
he likes to see in my black hair.

I will spread these flowers
over the square of earth he has chosen:
at the point where sky touches ground,
and a kapok tree has offered the man shade
for half a century.
            There, he has rested,
leaning against the time-smoothed trunk
to watch the wild parrots alight at dusk,
greening the branches like new leaves; there too,
he has listened to their murmurings
until the coming of night silenced them.

            Now he is waiting
to welcome me with wine and flowers.
He will take me into his arms and call me *Mi Vida:*
my life, *his* life. I will stay with him
until the sun rises.

Paciencia

The oldest woman in the village, Paciencia,
predicts the weather from the flight of birds:
Today, it will rain toads, she says,
squinting her face into a mystery of wrinkles
as she reads the sky—*tomorrow,*
it will be snakes.
                              Paciencia moves
with the grace of a ghost, walking unnoticed
down the roads lined with pleading eyes
and grasping hands, clothed in the invisibility
of her great age.
                              Paciencia sucks the meat of figs
with toothless gums; sleeps little—shuffling
through empty rooms at night, making order,
breathing in the dust
careless youth stirs up in passing.
She hums as she weaves an endless pattern
of intersecting lines; she cocks her head sometimes,
as if listening for her name in the wind—
the dance of her bones evident through paper-thin skin
as she works—like a bird trapped in a sack.

                              And Paciencia does
what Paciencia pleases, having outlived rules.
She washes the limbs of the dead tenderly as babies
being readied for a nap; comforts the widows.
And while the world around her flames and freezes,
she tends the graves of the ones she remembers,
bending closer to the earth, like an old tree,
giving shelter, giving shade.

Old Women

Little packages, oh yes,
all old women make little packages
and stow them under their beds.
> —José Donoso,
> *The Obscene Bird of Night*

Evidence of *a woman's hard life*
on faces lined with meaning
like the Rosetta Stone; a litany
of ailments, marks of fear, nights of pain, knowledge
of solitude, of shameful family secrets,
and the occasional ecstasy they dare you to decipher.

Stored under groaning mattresses are the remnants
of their lives wrapped in little packages, taped or
tied with string: wedding photos
jaundiced with age and humidity, of couples
standing stiff as corpses at the greatest distance
the frame will allow, of serious infants
held by women in severe dresses. In bundles,
sheaves of magazines becoming

one moist lump; balls of string, baby clothes of cracked satin
and ragged lace, shoes curling tongue to heel—homogenized,
all of it velvety to the touch,
turning in the thick air of wet coughs and tea,
the thing they all once were—paper to pulp, cloth to fiber,
ashes to ashes.

Old women sit like hens over their soft bundles,
nest and nursery of their last days, letting
the effluence of memory, its pungent odor
of decay work through the clogged channels
of their brains, presiding over their days
like an opium dream.

Corazón's Café

I

Corazón knew that she should go back to the apartment now. It was after closing time, and soon the street would be deserted. But she felt less alone here in the café, among the shelves that she and Manuel had stocked together, than she did in their apartment. It had been their home among the barrio neighbors who had also been their customers for ten years. Although she had often talked of moving to a house in the suburbs, especially after their store had started paying for itself, she knew that Manuel loved El Building for the same reasons that others claimed to hate it. It had vida. It was filled with the life energies of generations of other Island people; the stairs sagged from the weight of their burdens, and the walls had absorbed the smells of their food. El Building had become their country now. But Corazón did not know if she could call it home now that Manuel was gone.

Corazón was sitting behind the counter as if expecting a rush of customers at that hour. But what came to her were memories. From where she sat she could read the labels of cans that reminded her of Manuel's special way of doing things.

Habichuelas rojas, the cans of red kidney beans they stacked in a little pyramid. There were little sacks next to it holding the long grain rice that Puerto Ricans like to eat. The only logic that Manuel followed in stocking his shelves was based on his idea of what most people wanted to see in a barrio store: foods that go together arranged in interesting ways in one area: rice and beans, with plantains nearby, as well as cans of sliced breadfruit, pumpkin, and other side dishes to inspire more creative meals. The whole store was arranged in possible meal combinations. And there was the "international" section where imported goods for the other Latino customers were displayed

93

by nationality. Exotic canned products from Brazil, "Cuban" fruit drinks now bottled in Miami, black frijoles from Mexico, and assorted candies from several South American countries with curious names like Suspiros and Merengues.

Leaning over, she could smell the fresh coffee they kept in a can on the counter to serve free to customers. The aroma took her back to the time she had met Manuel.

II

It had been a hot afternoon on the Island. He came out to wait on her from where he had been grinding coffee beans behind the counter of el mercado Gonzalez when she had walked in, her face streaked with tears after a confrontation with her father. She had been sent to buy a bottle of Palo Viejo rum.

Manuel had put the bottle in a brown sack, never taking his eyes away from her face. He had touched her hand with his fingers as he handed it to her. Later, she had smelled the fresh coffee on her skin. She had avoided washing that hand all day because by bringing it to her nose, she could recall the pleasure of his touch.

And his face was beautiful. She had always thought that it was not right to say that of a man, but as a plain woman who always noticed beauty in others, she considered herself a fair judge of *la belleza*. And Manuel had a face as lovely as Jesus in those paintings where he is offering you His Sacred Heart. Manuel had a little beard then too (which he had grown to look older than his eighteen years when he had asked for the job at the store). But the beard only framed and softened his features. His eyes were almond-shaped with long eyelashes that made shadows on his cheeks when he looked down to figure an account for a customer. His lips were an invitation for a kiss: full and sensuous.

The most attractive thing about Manuel to Corazón was the fact that Manuel seemed to be unaware of his good looks. He worked twelve-hour days at the mercado, then he went home to help his wid-owed mother take care of the house and the little plot of land where she grew a few vegetables. They subsisted on Manuel's small salary and on the money his mother made by cooking for other people's parties. That is how Manuel had learned to cook, by helping his mother in the kitchen.

Corazón's situation was the reverse. Her mother had died in child-birth, leaving her to her older sister's care. Consuelo had been little more than a child herself when she had to take over the house. Their father was a heavy drinker, becoming more reclusive and bitter as he got older. He provided for his daughters, bringing in money from his job as foreman at the factory, but he seemed indifferent to their emo-tional needs. Anger and violence were always a possibility when he was home. "Go get me a pint of Palo Viejo," was his usual greeting to Corazón in the evening. By the time she was eighteen, the task had become an unbearable humiliation. But if it wasn't Corazón, it would have to be her sister, Consuelo, who was older and secretly engaged to a man who had warned her (or so Consuelo had told Corazón) that if her old man forced her to go buy rum, he would come over and beat him senseless. They did not want more violence at home, did they? And besides, at twenty-five years of age, Consuelo believed this was her last chance at marriage. Consuelo had prom-ised Corazón that she would wait until Corazón had finished high school, then she would marry and leave town.

Meeting Manuel gave Corazón hope and a plan for the future. She had loved him immediately. But he was so timid that she found herself directing the courtship. She started by going on any pretext to the mercado, where she practiced seducing him with her eyes. She gave him looks she had learned from the Mexican movies at the cinema. But he simply looked embarrassed and lowered his eyes in confusion. Since Corazón was well aware of the fact that she was not beautiful, at first she thought he was rejecting her in his own gentle way. But the attraction was real. She could detect the electrically charged space between them when he faced her across the counter.

He was just too shy to speak. Finally Corazón decided to take action. One day she slipped him a note with the money as she paid for the groceries. It simply said, *Manuel, meet me behind the mercado at nine tonight.* Then she left quickly before he could say no. It was a daring plan. She had to get Consuelo to help her carry it out.

After dinner their father usually sat alone in his room listening to the radio. Consuelo and Corazón were supposed to wash the dishes, make the beds, and occupy themselves with sewing, reading, or some other "quiet" activity until he declared that it was time for bed at around ten. He never came into their room, though, and it was possible for one of them to sneak out of the house through the window, which led directly to a thickly overgrown backyard. The banana trees, the huge breadfruit tree, and the assorted plants that their mother had once cultivated but were now like a forest provided great cover. From years of playing in that wilderness as children, they both knew their way to the road by moonlight. So far, it had been Consuelo who sneaked out to meet her man. This night, it would be Corazón. Consuelo expressed concern about her sister's decision, but she also told the radiant girl that love had made her almost beautiful that night. Corazón smiled ironically at the "almost beautiful" but felt too excited to allow her sister's words to hurt her as they usually did. Consuelo offered to brush Corazón's glossy black hair. It was the one thing Corazón was proud of—she had beautiful hair like their mother's. She examined her face carefully in the mirror. She did not think herself vain, but for Manuel, she wished she were prettier. Corazón's face was the result of the history of Puerto Rico. Her high cheekbones and oval eyes came from her father's Taino Indian and African ancestry. From her mother's forebears in Spain Corazón had received the long, thin nose, curly black hair, and lightened complexion that made her skin neither copper nor tan but somewhere in between. Corazón wished she were thinner; her large bosom made her look heavier than she was. She wished she looked more like her mother, who, like Consuelo, had been a tiny delicate-featured woman with porcelain skin. She knew this from the wedding picture her father had on his dresser. She had seen him stare at it for hours while he drank and listened to the old songs on his radio.

Corazón let herself out of the window with her sister's help.

"Remember, I will be expecting you in two hours," Consuelo had whispered to her. "And please, Corazón, don't . . ." She had started to lecture her about not doing anything foolish, anything she might regret, but Corazón had already turned away from her older sister and was plunging into the garden's shadows.

Manuel was waiting for her on the back steps of the store. Her own daring had made her feel reckless, and she leaned down and kissed his mouth. It tasted like a sweet, moist fruit straight from the tree of summer. He pulled her down on the cool cement steps next to him.

"Corazón," he spoke her name for the first time, "what shall we do?" She knew immediately what she would say, and it would always be that way. Manuel would ask her to make the important decisions, and she always would.

"Marry me," she said.

"I have to take care of my mother. She is not well, and she's only got me."

"We will take care of her together, Manuel." Corazón felt like someone who dives from a sinking ship into the ocean. She would do anything to be with this man. She felt a sense of destiny, *el destino*, a powerful force taking over her life.

That night they began to make plans. Corazón would finish her schooling that year, then they would announce their engagement. She found it easy to take the lead with Manuel. She placed her eager mouth on his, and he responded with a tenderness and passion she could control by merely wishing it. He seemed to gauge her needs and give her exact quantities of passion—no more, no less. He smiled and nodded as she began to make plans for their future, even that first night when they knew not much more about each other than what their bodies told them—that they wanted to be together more than they wanted anything else.

Manuel walked Corazón home, as far as the large tree at the edge of the overgrown garden. They held each other for a long time, then said a quiet good-night with promises of another meeting in a few nights. Corazón climbed through the window into the room, where she found Consuelo sobbing on her bed.

"What is it, Consuelo, what is wrong?" Corazón stroked her sister's hair. She feared something awful had happened in her house, since Consuelo was crying so hard that her whole body trembled in Corazón's arms. After a few minutes, Consuelo sat up in bed and laid her head on her sister's lap, letting Corazón wipe the tears from her face with her skirt.

"It's father. He found my letters to Gustavo and he is furious. Oh, Corazón. He called me out to the living room, and I had a terrible time explaining why you had not come out with me. I told him you were feverish and had taken medicine. But he was too angry to care about you. He wants Gustavo to come over tomorrow. I'm so afraid."

"How did he find the letters, Consuelo?" Corazón knew that their father avoided their private rooms, as he did most places and people that reminded him of his wife. He would not even allow flowers in the house, because she had always had things blossoming and growing in her home. His grief had turned him inside out, and he wore all his bitterness on the surface of his skin. He had withdrawn into his room with his bottle and treated his daughters like bad memories, avoiding looking at their faces, which were composites of his and his dead wife's, yet jealously guarding them.

"I had put them in my missal. I guess I left it out on the table by mistake. He must have seen the papers sticking out."

Corazón gently lifted her sister's face and looked deeply into her eyes. Rising from the bed, she walked to the dresser. She was quick to figure out that Consuelo had wanted the old man to find the letters. It was like her sister to manipulate events to suit her needs. Though Corazón loved Consuelo very much, she had sometimes felt hurt and offended by her sister's somewhat devious ways of getting what she wanted. It was as if, in having to accept the responsibilities of a widower's home and a young sister to take care of, Consuelo had decided she could never trust anyone to treat her fairly, so she kept secrets and maneuvered people. Now she was hurrying up her future before Corazón could get too much of a head start. Corazón knew what would happen in the next few days. A wedding date would be set for Consuelo and Gustavo to marry and thus save their father's dignity.

"Consuelo, I thought you were going to wait for me to finish school before you married Gustavo." Corazón's tone let her sister know what she suspected. Consuelo rose abruptly from the bed, wiping the last of her tears from her face.

"If you are old enough to be with a man, my dear little sister, you are old enough to take care of yourself."

That was the moment in the lives of the two sisters when Corazón began to understand that in matters of love for men, family loyalty takes second place. Consuelo's maternal concern for Corazón evaporated when she felt an encroachment on her right as the eldest to marry first. She had come to this conclusion while she waited for her younger sister to return from meeting her man.

The wedding was planned rapidly. It was to be a simple ceremony at home, since Don Emilio, their father, would not agree to attend a church wedding. The witness was their aunt, who brought flowers for the bride in spite of her brother's ban and cooked a meal for the groom's parents. The couple would stay with his family at first, then leave for New Jersey, where Gustavo had been offered a job as a mechanic by his godfather, who owned a garage. Consuelo was a beautiful bride, painful to her father's eyes, since she resembled his wife so much. Right after the priest said his final blessing, Don Emilio retired to his room and closed the door on the party. Corazón helped her sister change clothes for the one-night honeymoon in the nearest city of Ponce. Though there had been tension between them in the past weeks, she was grateful to her sister for all her years of devoted care. She stood behind Consuelo, who was sitting at her dresser, and helped her remove the little crown of fresh flowers, *azucenas*, white lilies from her hair.

"Be happy," she had said, and she had meant it.

But Corazón's life in her father's house without her sister for company became a daily torment. Right after work, the old man would lock himself in his room to drink, and he did not emerge until morning. He did not speak to Corazón except to order her to do something around the house or to send her to the store for his main needs in those dark days: cigarettes and rum. Feeling desperately alone, one night Corazón looked outside her window and decided to go toward the one point of light in the distance—Manuel's house.

She found her way there in almost total darkness. Manuel's mother's house stood alone outside of town, and the streetlights gave way to a dirt road long before their few acres of land began. Corazón stumbled and cut herself on sharp rocks, and once coming upon a creek, she fell into the shallow water before finding the stepping-stones by moonlight. When she arrived, she was hurt, bleeding, and soaked to the skin through her thin dress. The house loomed above her on stilts.

Corazón sat on the ground where she could see Manuel moving behind the translucent curtains like a figure in a dream. She was exhausted, and he seemed beyond her reach. She allowed herself to cry a little, as she watched him turn off the light and come to the window to close the shutters against the mosquitoes as he prepared for bed. Corazón ran to the house and stood under his startled eyes.

"Corazón!" He could not believe what he was seeing. But she just reached her arms up to him, and by leaning his body halfway out of the window, he reached her and pulled her into his room. Without speaking they came together in the dim room that smelled of the warm milk sweetened with cinnamon he drank each evening, of soap and man's cologne. He unbuttoned her dress and dried her with his soft cotton shirt, and he kneeled on the floor and removed her sandals. Then he lifted her up in his arms like a child and took her to his bed, where she shivered until he enfolded her body with his own.

He kept repeating her name, "Corazón, Corazón," as if he were talking to himself, warning himself to be gentle with her. He kissed her mouth until she trusted herself enough to kiss him back, and only when she let her body respond to his hands did he push himself gently into her. He was patient as she experienced first pain, then pleasure so intense that she laughed aloud in surprise. He said, "Hush, mi Corazón, Mamá's in there." He pointed toward the wall. Corazón felt afraid that his mother had heard them. But their desire was stronger than caution and they made love again, quietly, falling asleep exhausted when it was almost light outside.

Sleeping in Manuel's arms had come as naturally as breathing to Corazón. The first morning in his mother's house, however, began with her awakening alone in his room. She heard a woman's soft voice on the other side of the thin wall and Manuel's deeper voice responding. But she could not make out the words. She considered jumping out of the window and running back to her home. Perhaps she could sneak back into her room before her father noticed her absence.

As she hurriedly dressed in clothes that smelled of the muddy water with which they were splattered, Manuel walked in with a woman's bright yellow dress on his arm. He handed it to her. Smiling, he said: "My mother thinks it will fit you."

Corazón had never met anyone like Doña Serena. She was so thin that the veins on her arms could be seen through her skin like lines on a map. She wore her gray hair pulled back tightly in a bun. There was no trace of makeup on her face, which was vaguely reminiscent of Manuel's—in the darkness of the pupils and the high forehead. But she looked wispy and fragile—almost otherworldly.

Manuel had told Corazón that his mother was not well, yet both of them worked constantly. That first morning when Corazón had shyly walked out of Manuel's room wearing the yellow dress that was too tight on her, she had been greeted by Doña Serena at a table set for three. Without comment Doña Serena had motioned Corazón over to her and had kissed the fearful girl on the cheek. Over a delicious breakfast of homemade bread and guava jelly, mother and son had discussed their plans for the day, including the wedding. Early that morning Doña Serena had arranged for the priest to marry them that same day in a simple ceremony in her living room. On her way to talk to the priest, she had stopped by Corazón's father's house. Don Emilio had refused to talk to her, saying only that he did not want to hear anything that had to do with Consuelo or Corazón anymore. Doña Serena had packed a few things in a bag for the girl. The wedding would take place after Manuel got home from the bodega and before they cooked the three dozen pasteles that a new customer had ordered. Corazón had looked in amazement at the older woman, who spoke these things in a calm voice. She felt a sense of peace, sitting in that sunny kitchen with these two people she would now call her family. After his mother went into the kitchen, Manuel asked Corazón if she agreed to Doña Serena's plans. Corazón assured him that she had never been happier about anything in her life. It was as if she had a mother again to take care of her.

And though there was little money, the three of them could have lived happily enough except for two awful things that followed one another in rapid succession. During the first year of their marriage, Doña Serena had begun experiencing excruciating pains in her chest. At first she did not want to go to the doctor, but Corazón finally persuaded her by telling her that she too had reason to have an examination.

The older woman had become her confidante in the last six months. Though she spoke very little herself, she listened attentively for hours to Corazón's story of her own mother's early death and the bitterness of life with an alcoholic father. The two women worked together all day. In the morning they tended the little garden. In the afternoons they prepared giant pots of ingredients for the meat pies to be delivered to people's houses by Manuel when he came home. The late evenings belonged to the couple as Doña Serena watched her telenovelas, the soap operas that she loved, on a little television set in her room. The noise made by the TV gave the lovers enough freedom to enjoy each other in their room next to hers.

They made love with the window thrown wide open to the smells of the Island, all concentrated on Doña Serena's property—her little garden of herbs with the pungent oregano overwhelming all the other aromatic plants, the cayenne peppers, the cilantro, the tasty Puerto Rican coriander, the *pimientos y ajíes* that went into her condiments and permeated even the naked wood of the house with the smell of food cooked in her kitchen every day. The breeze blew through the trees that surrounded and protected the little plot of cultivated ground, and it too added a special fragrance from the papaya with its pendulous fruit hanging delicately from its slender branches, and the banana trees that, even when not laden with stalks of the fat little *guineitos niños* that are melt-in-the-mouth sweet when fried, still bore the leaves that the expert cook knows should be used to wrap food that is boiled—to add the final touch of taste and also to make food a gift to be unwrapped in celebration. Manuel whispered these things to her as they lay in each other's arms at night. She laughed gently at his love of cooking and his amazing knowledge of plants and food; not long before, she had believed these interests were strictly feminine, but his hands caressing her body were also a revelation of what a real man could be. He was a passionate lover but patient, teaching her how to attain the most pleasure from her body. Her body. It was suddenly a marvelous thing, her body; a source of pleasure to a beautiful man, and now she was carrying his child. After lovemaking she placed his hand on her abdomen. Half asleep, he said: "You are enjoying my cooking, Corazón," and, chuckling, "there is more woman here than I married."

Corazón smiled in the dark, her face buried in his neck. She was savoring the moment, postponing telling him until after she went with Doña Serena to her doctor the next day. There had been happiness followed by concern on the older woman's face as she had examined Corazón's belly. Doña Serena had been a midwife for many years, though she had given up the practice some time ago when her strength had started to fail her.

"What is it, what is the matter?" Corazón had perceived Doña Serena's anxiety as her hands traced the tight roundness of her womb.

"It may be nothing, Hija, just an old woman's apprehensions about her first grandchild, but I want you to promise me something."

"What, Doña Serena?" Corazón felt a cold shiver run down her spine, a sense that something was wrong.

"That you will not tell Manuel about your pregnancy yet. Tomorrow I will take you to my doctor for tests." She had taken Corazón's hand in hers. "It is best to make certain in these matters, *querida*, men do not like to be disappointed about babies."

"I will wait until tomorrow to tell Manuel," Corazón had promised, something like fear settling in her chest so that she had trouble breathing.

And as the afternoon passed in its slow way, as it does in the country when the days are hot and humid, Corazón forgot about her anxiety and talked to her mother-in-law about the future—a topic that Doña Serena never contributed much to, knowing that it was not for her, instead listening attentively, closely, trying to picture what she would not be around to see. Mainly they talked about Manuel, who was at the center of their lives then. He wanted to open his own store. He was dissatisfied with the strictly mercenary way that his boss ran the mercado, caring only for the profits. Manuel wanted, even back then, to offer people more than a place to buy their groceries; he wanted to create the ideal food store where he would teach his customers how to select each fruit and vegetable and how to cook them too. Doña Serena and Corazón smiled as they discussed Manuel's missionary commitment to his dream of a store. They also worried together about his health. Though it seldom happened, sometimes Manuel experienced shortness of breath and dizzy spells that drove him into a darkened room where he would lie on the floor until he regained control of his breathing. He made excuses for not seeing a doctor, but the women plotted about how to get him there. In her usual reticent way, Doña Serena did not say much, but Corazón intuited that the mother feared that whatever made her chest hurt as if a jagged blade was being thrust through her ribs could also be part of Manuel's problem. All that she put aside, though, after Corazón announced her pregnancy and especially after Doña Serena's expert midwife's hands had discovered a more imminent tragedy taking shape within Corazón's body.

The doctor confirmed it. The pregnancy would not come to full term. Neither would any other. Corazón's womb was incapable of sustaining a baby; it would not stretch to accommodate a living fetus even for the minimum time needed. She would never bear a live child. The doctor recommended an immediate abortion and hysterectomy. Corazón collapsed in Doña Serena's arms. And when Manuel came into her room at the hospital before she was taken to the operating room, she pretended to be asleep. She could not look at him.

He was more loving and tender with her after that. Once he said to her that she was all he wanted, that he was happier than he had ever been. But seeing that Corazón's grief was too overwhelming for words of consolation, he never mentioned their lost child again.

Doña Serena died in her bed. The doctor expressed surprise that she had not cried out. An artery had burst. The pain must have been so unbearable that she had lost consciousness, or else she had chosen to keep it to herself. Corazón secretly believed that Doña Serena had always borne more than anyone knew. She was the kind of woman who is called a *sufrida*—one who accepts pain and sacrifice as her lot *and* her privilege. While Manuel wept over his saintly mother, Corazón felt cheated. She was angry that another chance at a mother's love and companionship had been taken away from her and, most unfair of all, that she herself could never have a child to make her life complete. She looked at Manuel kneeling by the coffin, his shoulders shaking with sobs, and for the first time, she saw that she would now have to be strong for both of them. She would have to take him by the hand and lead him where he wanted to go in life. In her anger, Corazón also felt strength filling her with determination. He wanted a store of his own, but he had no idea how to get it. She would now have a lot of time on her hands. She would start planning a future for them. What else was there for her to do?

"Manuel." She offered him her hand. "It is time to go home now." And he got on his feet and followed her into their future.

III

Corazón wished she could move everything out of the store that night. She did not think she could stay in this place without Manuel. When Tito, the super, Doña Iris, Elenita from El Building, Joe Méndez, the lawyer, and old Don Cándido came by for their cup of coffee and their groceries, they would find the place as empty as the day she and Manuel had stepped in and Manuel had turned and hugged her. It had been just what he wanted: a blank canvas on which to create his dream of a store where both the body and the spirit could be nourished. Had that been ten years ago already?

It was nearly midnight. Corazón sat on her high stool behind the counter with only the security lights on. She allowed the tears to come. She felt so alone without the man she had loved and worked with for one brief decade. She should have made Manuel take better care of himself. After Doña Serena's funeral, she had made Manuel go to the doctor for a complete physical examination. Her worst fears had been confirmed. Like his mother, he suffered from a congenital heart defect: one of the valves was too small, it constricted the flow of blood during times of anxiety or stress. Surgery was advised but at very high risk. And of course, being young and full of energy at that time, Manuel had chosen to wait; there was always a reason: money, the right time—after they had saved enough to come to America, after they bought the store. It was as if he didn't want to know that his heart was failing him. Then two days ago, the sudden, swift coronary after unloading a truck with Inocencia. Corazón had watched the two men working like brothers, in silent camaraderie, as they always did, in perfect unison—Inocencia inside the truck, handing down boxes to Manuel, who stacked them in the back room of the store. Corazón had noticed the paleness of Manuel's skin and the heavy perspiration, though it was a cold day. But she had been busy waiting on customers in front. When she heard the truck drive away with Inocencia at the wheel—on its way back to Miami to pick up fresh produce from the Island—Corazón had gone to find Manuel and insist that he take a break. But he had already collapsed, as quietly as had his mother all those years before. Corazón knew CPR and worked feverishly to bring him back, shouting all the while for an ambulance. There was one customer in the store—the old man, who spoke no English but who managed to dial the number written on the bulletin board behind the counter. The ambulance arrived and took her and Manuel to an emergency room, where he was declared dead on arrival.

Inocencia would have to be told about Manuel's death. She had to be there when he arrived in the morning. More than anything else, except perhaps the wake scheduled at the Ramirez funeral home for the next day and following that, the funeral—where Corazón expected most of the population of the barrio to show up, and to have to stand up to all the condolences by people who loved Manuel— she hated to have to break the news to Inocencia.

She remembered the day the Peruvian Indian had first appeared at the store. They had been doing all the work themselves then, from stocking to waiting on customers ten hours a day, and Manuel was driving to the docks of New York and occasionally to Miami for the fresh Island products he insisted on having. They could not afford to hire help yet, with the store just barely breaking even as they established themselves in the barrio. People here were slow to trust newcomers and loyal to the old bodega, Cheo's place, which was really more a domino hall and package shop. The ice had been broken when Manuel and Cheo became friends and encouraged each other's customers to patronize both places. That was one of Manuel's gifts, in Corazón's eyes—he had the magic touch when it came to people. One morning Manuel drove up to the front of the store in the rental truck he had used to pick up stock in the city. As usual, Corazón got ready to help him unload. As she watched Manuel stack the cartons in the back, she noticed a man squatting in front of the front door, basically blocking her way. She observed him for a minute, trying to determine whether he looked suspicious and she should call the Paterson police. He looked like a statue carved in bronze, totally immobile, unblinking. He was wearing a heavy wool poncho that covered most of his compact body. His face was purely Indian: the sculpted cheekbones, long nose, and onyx eyes of the Inca. His age could have been anywhere from twenty to fifty. There were no lines to indicate the passing of time on this man's face. He watched Manuel as intently as Corazón watched *him*. Then, with a slow and fluid motion, he rose from his squatting position and approached the back of the truck. Although Corazón was ready to take action should he make any threatening move, the man simply stood there until Manuel raised his eyes and acknowledged him with a puzzled nod. He had not been aware of his presence; that was obvious to Corazón. Since Manuel was holding up an obviously heavy box of canned goods, the man extended his arms toward Manuel, Manuel passed the carton down, and the action was repeated again and again until the truck was unloaded. It was like a choreographed dance. Corazón did not see either man's lips move. No words had been exchanged between them. But by the time she unlocked the front door to let them in, Corazón knew they had an employee.

After the shelves had been stocked, the men went in the back to crush the cartons, and although Corazón strained to hear, all she could make out was an occasional chuckle from Manuel and murmurs that were impossible to decipher. When they finally emerged, the man had removed his poncho, and Corazón noticed how thin, almost emaciated he was, but strong-looking like a runner. The tendons in his arms were like brown cords. He was as small as a twelve-year-old boy, but he had the look of a man who had endured much.

"This is Inocencia Beleval, Corazón. He is from Peru."

Corazón almost extended her hand to the silent Inocencia, but he was looking down at the floor and not at her during the introduction. It was a gesture of respect, not humility. Corazón observed the almost imperceptible bow of the head, and how Inocencia looked directly into her husband's eyes after Manuel had spoken her name. It was all stated in silence: Inocencia acknowledged her as his boss's wife, but he worked for Manuel only. Corazón understood this and was a little irritated by it. The store belonged as much to her as to Manuel. In fact, she kept the books, paid the bills, and made all the decisions except those in the only area that really interested Manuel—the ordering of stock and its display in the store. But as the weeks passed and she saw how important Inocencia's quiet companionship was to Manuel, she began to feel differently about him. It was not a competition for Manuel's attention; Corazón noticed how inconspicuous Inocencia made himself when she was around. He was always busy in the back, organizing, sweeping, counting, and emerging only when she got busy with customers. Then he would simply do what needed to be done, from bagging to carrying groceries for old people or pregnant women across the street to El Building, where most of their customers lived. Corazón became curious as to what he did when he was not working, and she asked Manuel where Inocencia lived and whether he had a family. Manuel said that all he knew was that Inocencia had a room in a boardinghouse and that he had a wife and children in a mountain village in Peru. Apparently Inocencia had walked and hitched rides from Peru to Mexico, lived there for a while and then crossed over to the United States. He had made his way to New York by bus, then to Paterson after he found out that there were better job opportunities here. Manuel also admitted that Inocencia was not a United States citizen.

"But that could get us in trouble with the law, Manuel." Corazón had really felt frightened about having an illegal alien working for them. But Manuel had smiled mysteriously and opened his ledger, where he had a stack of documents with the United States Customs and Immigration seal on them.

"I have contacted an attorney, Corazón. The process has been started to make Inocencia a citizen. It will take some time, but we can do it."

"*We* can do it?" Corazón had felt offended that Manuel had done this without consulting her—the first time in their married lives that he had failed to confide in her. But she managed to keep her anger in check when she realized that Manuel wanted to do this for his friend without her help.

The men's friendship had grown and deepened. Corazón was aware of it and knew that perhaps Manuel was filling a need that she had not been able to fulfill in their lives: a son.

IV

The two years after Doña Serena's death had been years of hard work and sacrifice for Corazón and Manuel. Heartbroken, Manuel poured all his energies into the catering business which Corazón now directed from Doña Serena's house. Their goal was to save enough money to move to the states and open a store.

Reluctantly, Corazón had contacted her sister, Consuelo, now living with her husband in Paterson and expecting a child. It was Consuelo, lonely for her sister, who encouraged them to make the move. She would find them an apartment in the building where she lived. Corazón made herself believe that leaving the Island and starting a new life in America would help her get over the tragedy of being childless. At the end of two years, they had sold the little plot of land and house Doña Serena had left them and taken the airplane from San Juan to New York.

Corazón had not let her fear of the future show as they landed at La Guardia Airport nor as they rode in Gustavo's car through the labyrinthine city and across the gray Hudson River toward another maze of buildings which would be their new home. She and Manuel held hands in the back seat. At least they had each other.

Manuel had taken to barrio life quickly; she saw how the crowded apartment building everyone called El Building suited him. Each person he met was a future customer of his dream store. He became popular with the women because he spent time talking about food with them. The men liked him because he brought with him the dreams they had all had once and forgotten: to start a business in America, to prosper.

Corazón went with him to look for locations and soon they found the place they wanted. It had once been an Italian deli, and Manuel claimed that he could still smell in the wood the spices that had been sold there. It had "corazón y alma," he claimed, making a pun with her name, "heart and soul." So they had rented the place and Manuel had hired an unemployed artist from the Island to paint the sign on their window. He had not allowed Corazón to come to the place that day. He had wanted to surprise her. That night he took her to see the huge letters blocked in brilliant red: CORAZON'S CAFE. Under it there was a plump heart with the inscription "M ama C" in the middle. Manuel loves Corazón. She had cried. Manuel had his dream and she had him. What more could she ask for? She knew the answer to her own question. A child, a child. But she buried it deep in her heart that night as she stood in front of Corazón's Café. She was lucky enough.

Slowly the store had become part of the barrio. Manuel, Inocencia, and she worked as a team. There were good years and bad, but she had settled into a role that she had not foreseen. Some of the residents of El Building saw her as a confidante. It must have been the way she appeared, sitting behind the counter: a plump mother to everyone. She had gained weight—which Manuel said he liked: "The more of Corazón there is, the more of Corazón I love," he was fond of saying. A childless woman who knew how to keep secrets, she was unusual in the barrio where women married young, had more children than they could afford, and passed the time gossiping at each other's kitchen tables. Not everyone was like that, of course. Some of the young women graduated from high school and got good jobs and good places to live in the suburbs. She saw the changes that came over them. They were slim, spoke only English even when addressed in Spanish, and came to her store to buy Puerto Rican products only during holidays. The Island to them was an exotic place where their parents had been born long ago. Corazón listened to their mothers' laments about their hijas and *el olvido*. It was not hard for the young people to forget the barrio. Life there was hard. But, as Manuel liked to say, at least there was *life* in the barrio. To him the suburbs were a fancy prison where you went to retire from life. And so Corazón also learned to stop wanting her own house. After all, there was only the two of them. They didn't need much room. And besides, they spent ten to twelve hours a day in the store, going home only to sleep.

And her life had meaning—all the people who depended on her and Manuel to provide them with a taste of home. There was not a birth, funeral, or holiday celebrated in the barrio that they were not a part of: Manuel was never happier than when he was planning the food to celebrate life and never more beautiful in Corazón's eyes than when he comforted the grieving widow or orphan with food prepared with all the care and love he had to give. And she made it possible by doing all the work needed to make his labor of love easy for him. She learned to speak good English in order to deal with suppliers and creditors. She took accounting courses at night school and kept books. She paid bills and made telephone calls. They were a good team, she and Manuel.

But she had again been betrayed by El Destino. Fate had tricked her once more and taken away her man, her partner, her anchor in life. Corazón heard the clock's hands move—it was that quiet in the store. It was midnight.

V

She must have fallen asleep sometime during the night, her head cradled on her arms on the counter. When Corazón opened her eyes it was to find Inocencia outside the door, standing like a statue. She had no idea how long he had been there, but obviously he had seen her through the glass and not come in while she was asleep, although he had a key. She glanced at the wall clock as she hurried to open the front door. It was 5:45. They usually opened at six in order to serve coffee and pastries to those heading for work. Corazón mentally prepared for the day as she always had, even though she was also making plans to tell Inocencia that she was going to close Corazón's Café. She would ask Cheo to give the man a job. She was certain he would hire Inocencia. It had been a standard joke between Manuel and Cheo that Inocencia was the kind of worker you had to keep a secret or someone would steal him away. But it had been loyalty, not just the modest salary they were able to pay him, that had kept him at the café for eight years. Inocencia was now a United States citizen and had brought his wife and two teenage children to Paterson. Corazón had been surprised that he was old enough to have grown children. And she had developed a good relationship with his family too, although they, like Inocencia, kept very much to themselves. Manuel had been beside himself with joy when the official citizenship papers had come through. And it had been the one and only time when Corazón had heard Inocencia laugh aloud. She opened the door and helped Inocencia bring in the boxes of frozen pasteles, the banana leaves in iced containers for the women who preferred to make their own, and all the other holiday food that had to be driven from Miami up to Paterson for Thanksgiving and Christmas. She waited until the truck was empty and Inocencia was taking his usual break, sitting on a crate, smoking a cigar he had bought from a Cuban tobacconist: his only indulgence. Corazón then came into the storeroom.

In Spanish she said: "Inocencia, I have something important to tell you." He looked not at her but at the smoke rising in a spiral from the cigar in his hand.

"Manuel is dead. Muerto." The word was so powerful on her tongue that Corazón broke down in sobs. She covered her face, knowing that this would embarrass the shy and reserved Inocencia. But she felt a warm hand on her shoulder and uncovered her face. He had come closer and was standing in front of her, looking straight into her eyes. He too had tears streaming down his cheeks.

"Ya lo sé," he said. He knew it already. Before she could ask him how he knew, a loud knock came at the door. Without thinking, Corazón rushed to the front. It was six in the morning. Old Doña Iris, wrapped in a black shawl, was peering in the store through the glass. When Corazón unlocked the door, she saw that a small crowd had gathered in front. Doña Iris walked imperiously in as she always did but came directly toward Corazón, who had not yet assumed her place on the high stool behind the counter. The old woman hugged Corazón tightly, planted a loud kiss on her cheek, then demanded in her loud voice:

"Did my banana leaves come in? How am I going to make pasteles in time for Thanksgiving without the leaves?" And she headed for the freezer in the back of the store. The others came in more quietly, but each one of them stopped to embrace her. Her sister, Consuelo, and her niece, Cory, who was also Corazón's goddaughter, took their place next to her as her family while she received condolences from her neighbors and customers. Inocencia came out to help her make coffee and serve *pastelillos*, and Corazón listened to them talk about her Manuel. Even when everyone had left for their daily occupations, and Inocencia was in the back organizing and sweeping as he did every day, Corazón felt Manuel's presence in the store. Would the loneliness come back after he was laid to rest far away from the barrio? Could she bear to keep doing alone the things they had done together all these years? And there was still the empty apartment she would return to that night. Corazón allowed these questions to come and go as she waited on her customers that day. And when Roberto rushed in to say that Lydia had given birth to a little boy that morning and that she wanted more than anything else for Corazón to come see them at St. Joseph's Hospital and to bring her something sweet to eat, what could she do? She promised the excited young man that she would be there that afternoon. And when Don Candido came in, looking as old as Methuselah but still willing to proclaim his views on the world to anyone who would listen, she listened. He had lost two sons to ideology in Cuba. One fighting for Fidel and the other one, a poet the government did not approve of, languishing in a prison. Don Candido had made up his mind not to die before his son was freed. He kept himself alive by writing letters to judges, politicians, and the president and by talking and talking and talking. Corazón's Café was his forum and his refuge.

"¡*Libertad!*" Don Cándido waved a rolled-up newspaper at her as he headed for the coffeepot. And Corazón sat down to listen. He would drink several cups of espresso, talk about politics, read her a poem his son had written years ago before his imprisonment, and then leave—recharged—to visit his few surviving old friends, to talk away death for one more day.

The day passed quicker than she had expected, since each customer demanded her attention in a complete way. That afternoon she left the store in Inocencia's hands and took the bus to St. Joseph's Hospital. Lydia, whose mother had passed away from cancer, was waiting for her with the tiny bundle in her arms. She asked Corazón to hold him.

The baby had the face of a wise old man and a shock of black hair at the very top of his head. Corazón pronounced him beautiful. Roberto burst into the room with a bunch of flowers in his hands. He shouted from the door: "Is Manuel awake?"

Hearing her husband's name said with so much joy stunned Corazón. Lydia hurried to explain.

"I was just about to tell you, Corazón. We have decided to name our son Manuel."

"Manuel," Corazón said, and the tiny boy in her arms opened his eyes and began to cry for his mother.

That night Corazón and Inocencia closed Corazón's Café together and walked to El Building—he had accompanied her there without asking. He stood silently while she searched her purse for her apartment key. Knowing him as she did, Corazón knew he was waiting for her to say something.

"I will meet you at 5:30 tomorrow, Inocencia. We have a lot to do before the funeral." She had had to pause after the awful word, but Inocencia continued to listen as if he knew that her sentence was not finished—"and a lot to do before Thanksgiving and Christmas."

"Buenas noches, Doña Corazón." Inocencia had never spoken her name directly to her; he had always called Manuel *Don* Manuel although they were more like brothers than boss and employee.

"Buenas noches, *Don* Inocencia," Corazón replied and saw the brief smile pass over Inocencia's serious face before he nodded and disappeared around the corner. Corazón then entered El Building. At the bottom of the staircase, she took a deep breath, remembering Manuel's claim, that, simply from the lingering smells, he could tell her what each family in each apartment had had for dinner that evening and whether they had bought the condiments at Corazón's Café. Corazón inhaled deeply the aromas of her country and started the climb up to her home.

THE
MEDIUM'S
BURDEN

Tell all the Truth but tell it slant—
—Emily Dickinson

How to Get a Baby

To receive the *waiwaia* (spirit children) in the water seems to be the
most usual way of becoming pregnant. . . . They come along on large tree
trunks, and they may be attached to seascum and dead leaves floating on
the surface.

—Bronislaw Malinowski,
Baloma: The Spirits of the Dead in the Trobriand Islands

Go to the sea
the morning after a rainstorm,
preferably
fresh from your man's arms—
the *waiwaia* are drawn
to love smell.
They are tiny luminous fish
and blind. You must call
the soul of your child
in the name of your ancestors:
*Come to me, little fish, come
to Tamala, Tudava, come to me.*
Sit in shallow water
up to your waist until the tide
pulls away from you
like an exhausted lover.
You will by then
be carrying new life.
Make love that night,
and every night,
to let the little one
who chooses you know
she is one with your joy.

Advanced Biology

As I lay out my clothes for the trip to Miami to do a reading from my recently published novel, then on to Puerto Rico to see my mother, I take a close look at my travel wardrobe—the tailored skirts in basic colors easily coordinate with my silk blouses—I have to smile to myself, remembering what my mother had said about my conservative outfits when I visited her the last time—that I looked like the Jehovah's Witnesses who went from door to door in her pueblo trying to sell tickets to heaven to the die-hard Catholics. I would scare people, she said. They would bolt their doors if they saw me approaching with my briefcase. As for her, she dresses in tropical colors—a red skirt and parakeet yellow blouse look good on her tan skin, and she still has a good enough figure that she can wear a tight black cocktail dress to go dancing at her favorite club, El Palacio, on Saturday nights. And, she emphasizes, still make it to the ten o'clock mass on Sunday. Catholics can have fun and still be saved, she has often pointed out to me, but only if you pay your respects to God and all his court with the necessary rituals. She knows that over the years I have gradually slipped away from the faith in which I was so strictly brought up.

As I pack my clothes into the suitcase, I recall our early days in Paterson, New Jersey, where we lived for most of my adolescence while my father was alive and stationed in Brooklyn Yard in New York. At that time, our Catholic faith determined our family's views on most things, from clothing to the unmentioned subject of sex. Religion was the shield we had developed against the cold foreign city. These days we have traded places in a couple of areas since she has gone home to make a new life for herself after my father's death. I chose to attend college in the United States and make a living as an English teacher and, lately, on the lecture circuit as a novelist and poet. But though our lives are on the surface radically different, my mother and I have affected each other reciprocally over the past twenty years; she has managed to liberate herself from the rituals, mores, and traditions that "cramp" her style while retaining her femininity and "Puertoricanness," while I struggle daily to consolidate my opposing cultural identities. In my adolescence, divided into my New Jersey years and my Georgia years, I received an education in the art of cultural compromise.

In Paterson in the 1960s I attended a public school in our neighborhood. Still predominantly white and Jewish, it was rated very well academically in a city where the educational system was in chaos, deteriorating rapidly as the best teachers moved on to suburban schools following the black and Puerto Rican migration into, and the white exodus from, the city proper. The Jewish community had too much at stake to make a fast retreat; many of the small businesses and apartment buildings in the city's core were owned by Jewish families of the World War II generation. They had seen worse things happen than the influx of black and brown people that was scaring away the Italians and the Irish. But they too would gradually move their families out of the best apartments in their buildings and into houses in East Paterson, Fairlawn, and other places with *lawns*. It was how I saw the world then; either you lived without your square of grass, or you bought a house to go with it. But for most of my adolescence, I lived among the Jewish people of Paterson. We rented an apartment owned by the Milsteins, proprietors also of the deli on the bottom floor. I went to school with their children. My father took his business to the Jewish establishments, perhaps because these men symbolized "dignified survival" to him. He was obsessed with privacy and could not stand the personal turns conversations almost always took when two or more Puerto Ricans met casually over a store counter. The Jewish men talked too, but they concentrated on externals. They asked my father about his job, politics, his opinion on Vietnam, Lyndon Johnson. And my father, in his quiet voice, answered their questions knowledgeably. Sometimes before we entered a store, the cleaners, or a shoe repair shop, he would tell me to look for the blue-inked numbers on the owner's left forearm. I would stare at these numbers, now usually faded enough to look like veins in the wrong place. I would try to make them out. They were a telegram from the past, I later decided, informing the future of the deaths of millions. My father discussed the Holocaust with me in the same hushed tones my mother used to talk about God's Mysterious Ways. I could not reconcile both in my mind. This conflict eventually led to my first serious clash with my mother over irreconcilable differences between the "real world" and religious doctrine.

It had to do with the Virgin Birth.

And it had to do with my best friend and study partner, Ira Nathan, the acknowledged scientific genius at school. In junior high school it was almost a requirement to be "in love" with an older boy. I was an eighth grader and Ira was in the ninth grade that year and preparing to be sent away to some prep school in New England. I chose him as my boyfriend (in the eyes of my classmates, if a girl spent time with a boy, that meant they were "going together") because I needed tutoring in biology—one of his best subjects. I ended up having a crush on him after our first Saturday morning meeting at the library. Ira was my first exposure to the wonders of an analytical mind.

The problem was the subject. Biology is a dangerous topic for young teenagers, who are themselves walking laboratories, experimenting with interesting combinations of chemicals every time they make a choice. In my basic biology class, we were looking at single-cell organisms under the microscope, and watching them reproduce in slow-motion films in a darkened classroom. Though the process was as unexciting as watching a little kid blow bubbles, we were aroused by the concept itself. Ira's advanced class was dissecting fetal pigs. He brought me a photograph of his project, inner organs labeled neatly on the paper the picture had been glued to. My eyes refused to budge from the line drawn from "genitals" to a part of the pig to which it pertained. I felt a wave of heat rising from my chest to my scalp. Ira must have seen my discomfort, though I tried to keep my face behind the black curtain of my hair, but as the boy scientist, he was relentless. He actually traced the line from label to pig with his pencil.

"All mammals reproduce sexually," he said in a teacherly monotone.

The librarian, far off on the other side of the room, looked up at us and frowned. Logically, it was not possible that she could have heard Ira's pronouncement, but I was convinced that the mention of sex enhanced the hearing capabilities of parents, teachers, and librarians by 100 percent. I blushed more intensely, and peeked through my hair at Ira.

He was holding the eraser of his pencil on the pig's blurry sexual parts and smiling at me. His features were distinctly Eastern European. I had recently seen the young singer Barbra Streisand on the Red Skelton show and had been amazed at how much similarity there was in their appearances. She could have been his sister. I was particularly attracted to the wide mouth and strong nose. No one that I knew in school thought that Ira was attractive, but his brains had long ago overshadowed his looks as his most impressive attribute. Like Ira, I was a straight A student and also considered odd because I was one of the few Puerto Ricans on the honor roll. So it didn't surprise anyone that Ira and I had drifted toward each other. Though I could not have articulated it then, Ira was seducing me with his No. 2 pencil and the laboratory photograph of his fetal pig. The following Saturday, Ira brought in his advanced biology book and showed me the transparencies of the human anatomy in full color that I was not meant to see for a couple more years. I was shocked. The cosmic jump between paramecium and the human body was almost too much for me to take in. These were the first grown people I had ever seen naked, and they revealed too much.

"Human sexual reproduction can only take place when the male's sperm is introduced into the female womb and fertilization of the egg takes place," Ira stated flatly.

The book was open to the page labeled "The Human Reproductive System." Feeling that my maturity was being tested, as well as my intelligence, I found my voice long enough to contradict Ira.

"There has been one exception to this, Ira." I was feeling a little smug about knowing something that Ira obviously did not.

"Judith, there are no exceptions in biology, only mutations, and adaptations through evolution." He was smiling in a superior way.

"The Virgin Mary had a baby without . . ." I couldn't say *having sex* in the same breath as the name of the Mother of God. I was totally unprepared for the explosion of laughter that followed my timid statement. Ira had crumpled in his chair and was laughing so hard that his thin shoulders shook. I could hear the librarian approaching. Feeling humiliated, I started to put my books together. Ira grabbed my arm.

"Wait, don't go," he was still giggling uncontrollably. "I'm sorry. Let's talk a little more. Wait, give me a chance to explain."

Reluctantly, I sat down again, mainly because the librarian was already at our table, hands on hips, whispering angrily: "If you *children* cannot behave in this *study area*, I will have to ask you to leave." Ira and I both apologized, though she gave him a nasty look because his mouth was still stretched from ear to ear in a hysterical grin.

"Listen, listen. I'm sorry that I laughed like that. I know you're Catholic and you believe in the Virgin Birth" (he bit his lower lip trying to regain his composure), "but it's just not biologically possible to have a baby without" (he struggled for control) "losing your virginity."

I sank down on my hard chair. "Virginity." He had said another of the forbidden words. I glanced back at the librarian who was keeping her eye on us. I was both offended and excited by Ira's blasphemy. How could he deny a doctrine that people had believed in for two thousand years? It was part of my prayers every night. Our family talked about *La Virgen* as if she were our most important relative.

Recovering from his fit of laughter, Ira kept his hand discreetly on my elbow as he explained in the seductive language of the scientific laboratory how babies were made and how it was impossible to violate certain natural laws.

"Unless God wills it," I argued feebly.

"There is no God," said Ira, and the last shred of my innocence fell away as I listened to his arguments backed up by irrefutable scientific evidence.

Our meetings continued all that year, becoming more exciting with every chapter in his biology book. My grades improved dramatically, since one-celled organisms were no mystery to a student of advanced biology. Ira's warm, moist hand often brushed against mine under the table at the library, and walking home one bitter cold day, he asked me if I would wear his Beta Club pin. I nodded, and when we stepped inside the hallway of my building, where he removed his thick mittens which his mother had knitted, he pinned the blue enamel B to my collar. And to the hissing of the steam heaters, I received a serious kiss from Ira. We separated abruptly when we heard Mrs. Milstein's door open.

"Hello, Ira."

"Hello, Mrs. Milstein."

"And how is your mother? I haven't seen Fritzie all week. She's not sick, is she?"

"She's had a mild cold, Mrs. Milstein. But she is steadily improving." Ira's diction became extremely precise and formal when he was in the presence of adults. As an only child and a prodigy, he had to live up to very high standards.

"I'll call her today," Mrs. Milstein said, finally looking over at me. Her eyes fixed on the collar of my blouse which was, I later saw in our hall mirror, sticking straight up with Ira's pin attached crookedly to the edge.

"Good-bye, Mrs. Milstein."

"Nice to see you, Ira."

Ira waved awkwardly to me as he left. Mrs. Milstein stood in the humid hallway of her building, watching me run up the stairs.

Our "romance" lasted only a week; long enough for Mrs. Milstein to call Ira's mother and for Mrs. Nathan to call my mother. I was subjected to a lecture on moral behavior by my mother, who, carried away by her anger and embarrassed that I had been seen kissing a boy (understood: a boy who was not even Catholic), had begun reciting a litany of metaphors for the loss of virtue.

"A cheap item," she said trembling before me as I sat on the edge of my bed, facing her accusations, "a girl begins to look like one when she allows herself to be *handled* by men."

"Mother . . ." I wanted her to lower her voice so that my father, sitting at the kitchen table, reading, would not hear. I had already promised her that I would confess my sin that Saturday and take communion with a sparkling clean soul. I had not been successful at keeping the sarcasm out of my voice. Her fury was fueled by her own bitter catalogue.

"A burden to her family . . ." She was rolling with her Spanish now. Soon the Holy Mother would enter into the picture for good measure. "It's not as if I had not taught you better. Don't you know that those people do not have the example of the Holy Virgin Mary and her Son to follow, and that is why they do things for the wrong reasons? Mrs. Nathan said she did not want her son messing around with you—not because of the wrongness of it—but because it would interfere with his studies!" She was yelling now. "She's afraid that he will" (she crossed herself at the horror of the thought) "make you pregnant!"

"We could say an angel came down and put a baby in my stomach, Mother." She had succeeded in dragging me into her field of hysteria.

"I do not want you associating any more than necessary with people who do not have God, do you hear me?"

"They have a god!" I was screaming now too, trying to get away from her: "They have an intelligent god who doesn't ask you to believe that a woman can get pregnant without having sex!"

"Nazi," I hissed, "I bet you'd like to send Ira and his family to a concentration camp!" At that time I thought that was the harshest thing I could have said to anyone. I was certain that I had sentenced my soul to eternal damnation the minute the words came out of my mouth: but I was so angry I wanted to hurt her.

Father walked into my room at that moment, looking shocked at the sight of the two of us entangled in mortal combat.

"Please, please," his voice sounded agonized. I ran to him, and he held me in his arms while I cried my heart out on his starched white shirt. My mother, also weeping quietly, tried to walk past us, but he pulled her into the circle. After a few moments, she put her trembling hand on my head.

"We are a family," my father said, "there is just us against the world. Please, please . . ." But he did not follow the "please" with any suggestions as to what we could do to make things right in a world that was as confusing to my mother as it was to me.

I finished the eighth grade in Paterson, but Ira and I never got together to study again. I sent his Beta Club pin back to him via a mutual friend. Once in a while I saw him in the hall or the playground. But he seemed to be in the clouds, where he belonged. In the fall, I was enrolled at the Catholic high school where everyone believed in the Virgin Birth, and I never had to take a test on the human reproductive system. It was a chapter that was not emphasized.

In 1968, my father retired from the navy and began looking for a better place for us to live. He decided to move us to Augusta, Georgia, where he had relatives who had settled after retiring from the army at Fort Gordon. They had convinced him that it was a healthier place to rear teenagers. For me it was a shock to the senses, like moving from one planet to another: where Paterson had concrete to walk on and gray skies, bitter winters, and a smorgasbord of an ethnic population, Georgia was red like Mars, and Augusta was green—exploding in colors in more gardens of azaleas and dogwood and magnolia trees—more vegetation than I imagined was possible anywhere not tropical like Puerto Rico. People seemed to come in two basic colors: black and blond. And I could barely understand my teachers when they talked in a slowed-down version of English like one of those old 78-speed recordings played at 33. But I was placed in all advanced classes, and one of them was biology. This is where I got to see my first real fetal pig, which my assigned lab partner had chosen. She picked it up gingerly by the ends of the plastic bag in which it was stored: "Ain't he cute?" she asked. I nodded, nearly fainting from the overwhelming combination of the smell of formaldehyde and my sudden flashback to my brief but intense romance with Ira Nathan.

"What you want to call him?"

My partner unwrapped our specimen on the table, and I surprised myself by my instant recall of Ira's chart. I knew all the parts. In my mind's eye I saw the pencil lines, the labeled photograph. I had had an excellent teacher.

"Let's call him Ira."

"That's a funny name, but OK." My lab partner, a smart girl destined to become my mentor in things southern, then gave me a conspiratorial wink and pulled out a little perfume atomizer from her purse. She sprayed Ira from snout to tail with it. I noticed this operation was taking place at other tables too. The teacher had conveniently left the room a few minutes before. I was once again stunned—almost literally knocked out by a fist of smell:

"What is it?"

"*Intimate*," my advanced biology partner replied, smiling.

And by the time our instructor came back to the room, we were ready to delve into this mystery of muscle and bone; eager to discover the secrets that lie just beyond fear and a little past loathing; acknowledging the corruptibility of the flesh and our own fascination with the subject.

As I finish packing, the telephone rings and it's my mother. She is reminding me to be ready to visit relatives, to go to a dance with her, and of course, to attend a couple of the services at the church. It is the feast of the Black Virgin, revered patron saint of our home town in Puerto Rico. I agree to everything and find myself anticipating the eclectic itinerary. Why not allow Evolution and Eve, Biology and the Virgin Birth? Why not take a vacation from logic? I will not be away for too long, I will not let myself be tempted to remain in the sealed garden of blind faith; I'll stay just long enough to rest myself from the exhausting enterprise of leading the examined life.

The Paterson Public Library

It was a Greek temple in the ruins of an American city. To get to it I had to walk through neighborhoods where not even the carcasses of rusted cars on blocks nor the death traps of discarded appliances were parted with, so that the yards of the borderline poor, people who lived not in a huge building, as I did, but in their own decrepit little houses, looked like a reversed archaeological site, incongruous next to the pillared palace of the Paterson Public Library.

The library must have been built during Paterson's boom years as the model industrial city of the North. Enough marble was used in its construction to have kept several Michelangelos busily satisfied for a lifetime. Two roaring lions, taller than a grammar school girl, greeted those brave enough to seek answers there. Another memorable detail about the façade of this important place to me was the phrases carved deeply into the walls—perhaps the immortal words of Greek philosophers—I could not tell, since I was developing astigmatism at that time and could only make out the lovely geometric designs they made.

All during the school week I both anticipated and feared the long walk to the library because it took me through enemy territory. The black girl Lorraine, who had chosen me to hate and terrorize with threats at school, lived in one of the gloomy little houses that circled the library like beggars. Lorraine would eventually carry out her violence against me by beating me up in a confrontation formally announced through the school grapevine so that for days I lived with a panic that has rarely been equaled in my adult life, since now I can get grown-ups to listen to me, and at that time disasters had to be a fait accompli for a teacher or a parent to get involved. Why did Lorraine hate me? For reasons neither one of us fully understood at the time. All I remember was that our sixth grade teacher seemed to favor me, and her way of showing it was by having me tutor "slow" students in spelling and grammar. Lorraine, older and bigger than myself, since she was repeating the grade, was subjected to this ritual humiliation, which involved sitting in the hallway, obviously separated from the class—one of us for being smart, the other for the opposite reason. Lorraine resisted my efforts to teach her the basic rules of spelling. She would hiss her threats at me, addressing me as *You little spic.* Her hostility sent shudders through me. But baffling as it was, I also accepted it as inevitable. She would beat me up. I told my mother and the teacher, and they both reassured me in vague adult terms that a girl like Lorraine would not dare get in trouble again. She had a history of problems that made her a likely candidate for reform school. But Lorraine and I knew that the violence she harbored had found a target: me—the skinny Puerto Rican girl whose father was away with the navy most of the time and whose mother did not speak English; I was the perfect choice.

Thoughts like these occupied my mind as I walked to the library on Saturday mornings. But my need for books was strong enough to propel me down the dreary streets with their slush-covered sidewalks and the skinny trees of winter looking like dark figures from a distance: angry black girls waiting to attack me.

But the sight of the building was enough to reassure me that sanctuary was within reach. Inside the glass doors was the inexhaustible treasure of books, and I made my way through the stacks like the beggar invited to the wedding feast. I remember the musty, organic smell of the library, so different from the air outside. It was the smell of an ancient forest, and since the first books that I read for pleasure were fairy tales, the aroma of transforming wood suited me as a prop.

With my pink library card I was allowed to check out two books from the first floor—the children's section. I would take the full hour my mother had given me (generously adding fifteen minutes to get home before she sent my brother after me) to choose the books I would take home for the week. I made my way first through the world's fairy tales. Here I discovered that there is a Cinderella in every culture, that she didn't necessarily have the white skin and rosy cheeks Walt Disney had given her, and that the prince they all waited for could appear in any color, shape, or form. The prince didn't even have to be a man.

It was the way I absorbed fantasy in those days that gave me the sense of inner freedom, a feeling of power and the ability to fly that is the main reward of the writer. As I read those stories I became not only the characters but their creator. I am still fascinated by the idea that fairy tales and fables are part of humankind's collective unconscious—a familiar theory that acquires concreteness in my own writing today, when I discover over and over that the character I create or the themes that recur in my poems and in my fiction are my own versions of the "types" I learned to recognize very early in my life in fairy tales.

There was also violence in these stories: villains decapitated in honorable battle, goblins and witches pursued, beaten, and burned at the stake by heroes with magic weapons, possessing the supernatural strength granted to the self-righteous in folklore. I understood those black-and-white duels between evil and justice. But Lorraine's blind hatred of my person and my knee-liquefying fear of her were not so clear to me at that time. It would be many years before I learned about the politics of race, before I internalized the awful reality of the struggle for territory that underscored the lives of blacks and Puerto Ricans in Paterson during my childhood. Each job given to a light-skinned Hispanic was one less job for a black man; every apartment leased to a Puerto Rican family was one less place available to blacks. Worst of all, though the Puerto Rican children had to master a new language in the schools and were often subjected to the scorn and impatience of teachers burdened with too many students making too many demands in a classroom, the blacks were obviously the ones singled out for "special" treatment. In other words, whenever possible they were assigned to special education classes in order to relieve the teacher's workload, mainly because their black English dialect sounded "ungrammatical" and "illiterate" to our white Seton

Hall University and City College–educated instructors. I have on occasion become angry at being treated like I'm mentally deficient by persons who make that prejudgment upon hearing an unfamiliar accent. I can only imagine what it must have been like for children like Lorraine, whose skin color alone put her in a pigeonhole she felt she had to fight her way out of every day of her life.

I was one of the lucky ones; as an insatiable reader I quickly became more than adept at the use of the English language. My life as a navy brat, moving with my family from Paterson to Puerto Rico every few months as my father's tours of duty demanded, taught me to depend on knowledge as my main source of security. What I learned from books borrowed from the Greek temple among the ruins of the city I carried with me as the lightest of carry-on luggage. My teachers in both countries treated me well in general. The easiest way to become a teacher's pet, or *la favorita*, is to ask the teacher for books to read—and I was always looking for reading material. Even my mother's romantic novels by Corín Tellado and her *Buen-hogar* (Spanish *Good Housekeeping* magazine) were not safe from my insatiable word hunger.

Since the days when I was stalked by Lorraine, libraries have always been an adventure for me. Fear of an ambush is no longer the reason why I feel my pulse quicken a little when I approach a library building, when I enter the stacks and inhale the familiar smell of old leather and paper. It may be the memory of the danger that heightens my senses, but it is really the expectation that I felt then and that I still feel now about books. They contained most of the information I needed to survive in two languages and in two worlds. When adults were too busy to answer my endless questions, I could always *look it up*; when I felt unbearably lonely, as I often did during those early gypsy years traveling with my family, I read to escape and also to connect: you can come back to a book as you cannot always to a person or place you miss. I read and reread favorite books until the characters seemed like relatives or friends I could see when I wanted or needed to see them.

I still feel that way about books. They represent my spiritual life. A library is my sanctuary, and I am always at home in one. It is not surprising that in recalling my first library, the Paterson Public Library, I have always described it as a temple.

Lorraine carried out her threat. One day after school, as several of our classmates, Puerto Rican and black, circled us to watch, Lorraine grabbed a handful of my long hair and forced me to my knees. Then she slapped my face hard enough that the sound echoed off the brick walls of the school building and ran off while I screamed at the sight of blood on my white knee socks and felt the throbbing on my scalp where I would have a bald spot advertising my shame for weeks to come.

No one intervened. To this crowd, it was one of many such violent scenes taking place among the adults and the children of people fighting over a rapidly shrinking territory. It happens in the jungle and it happens in the city. But another course of action other than "fight or flight" is open to those of us lucky enough to discover it, and that is channeling one's anger and energy into the development of a mental life. It requires something like obsessiveness for a young person growing up in an environment where physical labor and physical endurance are the marks of a survivor—as is the case with minority peoples living in large cities. But many of us do manage to discover books. In my case, it may have been what anthropologists call a cultural adaptation. Being physically small, non-English-speaking, and always the new kid on the block, I was forced to look for an alternative mode to survival in Paterson. Reading books empowered me.

Even now, a visit to the library recharges the batteries in my brain. Looking through the card catalog reassures me that there is no subject that I cannot investigate, no world I cannot explore. Everything that is is mine for the asking. Because I can read about it.

The Story of My Body

Migration is the story of my body.
—Víctor Hernández Cruz

Skin

I was born a white girl in Puerto Rico but became a brown girl when I came to live in the United States. My Puerto Rican relatives called me tall; at the American school, some of my rougher classmates called me Skinny Bones, and the Shrimp because I was the smallest member of my classes all through grammar school until high school, when the midget Gladys was given the honorary post of front row center for class pictures and scorekeeper, bench warmer, in P.E. I reached my full stature of five feet in sixth grade.

I started out life as a pretty baby and learned to be a pretty girl from a pretty mother. Then at ten years of age I suffered one of the worst cases of chicken pox I have ever heard of. My entire body, including the inside of my ears and in between my toes, was covered with pustules which in a fit of panic at my appearance I scratched off my face, leaving permanent scars. A cruel school nurse told me I would always have them—tiny cuts that looked as if a mad cat had plunged its claws deep into my skin. I grew my hair long and hid behind it for the first years of my adolescence. This was when I learned to be invisible.

Color

In the animal world it indicates danger: the most colorful creatures are often the most poisonous. Color is also a way to attract and seduce

135

a mate. In the human world color triggers many more complex and often deadly reactions. As a Puerto Rican girl born of "white" parents, I spent the first years of my life hearing people refer to me as *blanca*, white. My mother insisted that I protect myself from the intense island sun because I was more prone to sunburn than some of my darker, *trigueño* playmates. People were always commenting within my hearing about how my black hair contrasted so nicely with my "pale" skin. I did not think of the color of my skin consciously except when I heard the adults talking about complexion. It seems to me that the subject is much more common in the conversation of mixed-race peoples than in mainstream United States society, where it is a touchy and sometimes even embarrassing topic to discuss, except in a political context. In Puerto Rico I heard many conversations about skin color. A pregnant woman could say, "I hope my baby doesn't turn out *prieto*" (slang for "dark" or "black") "like my husband's grandmother, although she was a good-looking *negra* in her time." I am a combination of both, being olive-skinned—lighter than my mother yet darker than my fair-skinned father. In America, I am a person of color, obviously a Latina. On the Island I have been called everything from a *paloma blanca*, after the song (by a black suitor), to *la gringa*.

My first experience of color prejudice occurred in a supermarket in Paterson, New Jersey. It was Christmastime, and I was eight or nine years old. There was a display of toys in the store where I went two or three times a day to buy things for my mother, who never made lists but sent for milk, cigarettes, a can of this or that, as she remembered from hour to hour. I enjoyed being trusted with money and walking half a city block to the new, modern grocery store. It was owned by three good-looking Italian brothers. I liked the younger one with the crew-cut blond hair. The two older ones watched me and the other Puerto Rican kids as if they thought we were going to steal something. The oldest one would sometimes even try to hurry me with my purchases, although part of my pleasure in these expeditions came from looking at everything in the well-stocked aisles. I was also teaching myself to read English by sounding out the labels in packages: L&M cigarettes, Borden's homogenized milk, Red Devil potted ham, Nestle's chocolate mix, Quaker oats, Bustelo coffee, Wonder bread, Colgate toothpaste, Ivory soap, and Goya (makers of products used in Puerto Rican dishes) everything—these are some of the brand names that taught me nouns. Several times this man had come up to me, wearing his blood-stained butcher's apron, and towering over me had asked in a harsh voice whether there was something he could help me find. On the way out I would glance at the younger brother who ran one of the registers and he would often smile and wink at me.

It was the mean brother who first referred to me as "colored." It was a few days before Christmas, and my parents had already told my brother and me that since we were in Los Estados now, we would get our presents on December 25 instead of Los Reyes, Three Kings Day, when gifts are exchanged in Puerto Rico. We were to give them a wish list that they would take to Santa Claus, who apparently lived in the Macy's store downtown—at least that's where we had caught a glimpse of him when we went shopping. Since my parents were timid about entering the fancy store, we did not approach the huge man in the red suit. I was not interested in sitting on a stranger's lap anyway. But I did covet Susie, the talking schoolteacher doll that was displayed in the center aisle of the Italian brothers' supermarket. She talked when you pulled a string on her back. Susie had a limited repertoire of three sentences: I think she could say: "Hello, I'm Susie Schoolteacher," "Two plus two is four," and one other thing I cannot remember. The day the older brother chased me away, I was reaching to touch Susie's blonde curls. I had been told many times, as most children have, not to touch anything in a store that I was not buying. But I had been looking at Susie for weeks. In my mind, she was my doll. After all, I had put her on my Christmas wish list. The moment is frozen in my mind as if there were a photograph of it on file. It was not a turning point, a disaster, or an earth-shaking revelation. It was simply the first time I considered—if naively—the meaning of skin color in human relations.

I reached to touch Susie's hair. It seems to me that I had to get on tiptoe, since the toys were stacked on a table and she sat like a princess on top of the fancy box she came in. Then I heard the booming "Hey, kid, what do you think you're doing!" spoken very loudly from the meat counter. I felt caught, although I knew I was not doing anything criminal. I remember not looking at the man, but standing there, feeling humiliated because I knew everyone in the store must have heard him yell at me. I felt him approach, and when I knew he was behind me, I turned around to face the bloody butcher's apron. His large chest was at my eye level. He blocked my way. I started to run out of the place, but even as I reached the door I heard him shout after me: "Don't come in here unless you gonna buy something. You PR kids put your dirty hands on stuff. You always look dirty. But maybe dirty brown is your natural color." I heard him laugh and someone else too in the back. Outside in the sunlight I looked at my hands. My nails needed a little cleaning as they always did, since I liked to paint with watercolors, but I took a bath every night. I thought the man was dirtier than I was in his stained apron. He was also always sweaty—it showed in big yellow circles under his shirt-sleeves. I sat on the front steps of the apartment building where we lived and looked closely at my hands, which showed the only skin I could see, since it was bitter cold and I was wearing my quilted play coat, dungarees, and a knitted navy cap of my father's. I was not pink like my friend Charlene and her sister Kathy, who had blue eyes and light brown hair. My skin is the color of the coffee my grandmother made, which was half milk, *leche con café* rather than *café con leche*. My mother is the opposite mix. She has a lot of café in her color. I could not understand how my skin looked like dirt to the supermarket man.

I went in and washed my hands thoroughly with soap and hot water, and borrowing my mother's nail file, I cleaned the crusted watercolors from underneath my nails. I was pleased with the results. My skin was the same color as before, but I knew I was clean. Clean enough to run my fingers through Susie's fine gold hair when she came home to me.

Size

My mother is barely four feet eleven inches in height, which is average for women in her family. When I grew to five feet by age twelve, she was amazed and began to use the word tall to describe me, as in "Since you are tall, this dress will look good on you." As with the color of my skin, I didn't consciously think about my height or size until other people made an issue of it. It is around the preadolescent years that in America the games children play for fun become fierce competitions where everyone is out to "prove" they are better than others. It was in the playground and sports fields that my size-related problems began. No matter how familiar the story is, every child who is the last chosen for a team knows the torment of waiting to be called up. At the Paterson, New Jersey, public schools that I attended, the volleyball or softball game was the metaphor for the battlefield of life to the inner city kids—the black kids versus the Puerto Rican kids, the whites versus the blacks versus the Puerto Rican kids; and I was 4F, skinny, short, bespectacled, and apparently impervious to the blood thirst that drove many of my classmates to play ball as if their lives depended on it. Perhaps they did. I would rather be reading a book than sweating, grunting, and running the risk of pain and injury. I simply did not see the point in competitive sports. My main form of exercise then was walking to the library, many city blocks away from my barrio.

Still, I wanted to be wanted. I wanted to be chosen for the teams. Physical education was compulsory, a class where you were actually given a grade. On my mainly all A report card, the C for compassion I always received from the P.E. teachers shamed me the same as a bad grade in a real class. Invariably, my father would say: "How can you make a low grade for *playing games?*" He did not understand. Even if I had managed to make a hit (it never happened) or get the ball over that ridiculously high net, I already had a reputation as a "shrimp," a hopeless nonathlete. It was an area where the girls who didn't like me for one reason or another—mainly because I did better than they on academic subjects—could lord it over me; the playing field was the place where even the smallest girl could make me feel powerless and inferior. I instinctively understood the politics even then; how the *not* choosing me until the teacher forced one of the team captains to call my name was a coup of sorts—there, you little show-off, tomorrow you can beat us in spelling and geography, but this afternoon you are the loser. Or perhaps those were only my own bitter thoughts as I sat or stood in the sidelines while the big girls were grabbed like fish and I, the little brown tadpole, was ignored until Teacher looked over in my general direction and shouted, "Call Ortiz," or, worse, "Somebody's *got* to take her."

No wonder I read Wonder Woman comics and had Legion of Super Heroes daydreams. Although I wanted to think of myself as "intellectual," my body was demanding that I notice it. I saw the little swelling around my once-flat nipples, the fine hairs growing in secret places; but my knees were still bigger than my thighs, and I always wore long- or half-sleeve blouses to hide my bony upper arms. I wanted flesh on my bones—a thick layer of it. I saw a new product advertised on TV. Wate-On. They showed skinny men and women before and after taking the stuff, and it was a transformation like the ninety-seven-pound-weakling-turned-into-Charles-Atlas ads that I saw on the back covers of my comic books. The Wate-On was very expensive. I tried to explain my need for it in Spanish to my mother, but it didn't translate very well, even to my ears—and she said with a tone of finality, eat more of my good food and you'll get fat—anybody can get fat. Right. Except me. I was going to have to join a circus someday as Skinny Bones, the woman without flesh.

Wonder Woman was stacked. She had a cleavage framed by the

spread wings of a golden eagle and a muscular body that has become fashionable with women only recently. But since I wanted a body that would serve me in P.E., hers was my ideal. The breasts were an indulgence I allowed myself. Perhaps the daydreams of bigger girls were more glamorous, since our ambitions are filtered through our needs, but I wanted first a powerful body. I daydreamed of leaping up above the gray landscape of the city to where the sky was clear and blue, and in anger and self-pity, I fantasized about scooping my enemies up by their hair from the playing fields and dumping them on a barren asteroid. I would put the P.E. teachers each on their own rock in space too, where they would be the loneliest people in the universe, since I knew they had no "inner resources," no imagination, and in outer space, there would be no air for them to fill their deflated volleyballs with. In my mind all P.E. teachers have blended into one large spiky-haired woman with a whistle on a string around her neck and a volleyball under one arm. My Wonder Woman fantasies of revenge were a source of comfort to me in my early career as a shrimp.

I was saved from more years of P.E. torment by the fact that in my sophomore year of high school I transferred to a school where the midget, Gladys, was the focal point of interest for the people who must rank according to size. Because her height was considered a handicap, there was an unspoken rule about mentioning size around Gladys, but of course, there was no need to say anything. Gladys knew her place: front row center in class photographs. I gladly moved to the left or to the right of her, as far as I could without leaving the picture completely.

Looks

Many photographs were taken of me as a baby by my mother to send to my father, who was stationed overseas during the first two years of my life. With the army in Panama when I was born, he later traveled often on tours of duty with the navy. I was a healthy, pretty baby. Recently, I read that people are drawn to big-eyed round-faced creatures, like puppies, kittens, and certain other mammals and marsupials, koalas, for example, and, of course, infants. I was all eyes, since my head and body, even as I grew older, remained thin and small-boned. As a young child I got a lot of attention from my relatives and many other people we met in our barrio. My mother's beauty may have had something to do with how much attention we got from strangers in stores and on the street. I can imagine it. In the pictures I have seen of us together, she is a stunning young woman by Latino standards: long, curly black hair, and round curves in a compact frame. From her I learned how to move, smile, and talk like an attractive woman. I remember going into a bodega for our groceries and being given candy by the proprietor as a reward for being *bonita*, pretty.

I can see in the photographs, and I also remember, that I was dressed in the pretty clothes, the stiff, frilly dresses, with layers of crinolines underneath, the glossy patent leather shoes, and, on special occasions, the skull-hugging little hats and the white gloves that were popular in the late fifties and early sixties. My mother was proud of my looks, although I was a bit too thin. She could dress me up like a doll and take me by the hand to visit relatives, or go to the Spanish mass at the Catholic church, and show me off. How was I to know that she and the others who called me "pretty" were representatives of an aesthetic that would not apply when I went out into the mainstream world of school?

In my Paterson, New Jersey, public schools there were still quite a few white children, although the demographics of the city were changing rapidly. The original waves of Italian and Irish immigrants, silk-mill workers, and laborers in the cloth industries had been "assimilated." Their children were now the middle-class parents of my peers. Many of them moved their children to the Catholic schools that proliferated enough to have leagues of basketball teams. The names I recall hearing still ring in my ears: Don Bosco High versus

St. Mary's High, St. Joseph's versus St. John's. Later I too would be transferred to the safer environment of a Catholic school. But I started school at Public School Number 11. I came there from Puerto Rico, thinking myself a pretty girl, and found that the hierarchy for popularity was as follows: pretty white girl, pretty Jewish girl, pretty Puerto Rican girl, pretty black girl. Drop the last two categories; teachers were too busy to have more than one favorite per class, and it was simply understood that if there was a big part in the school play, or any competition where the main qualification was "present-ability" (such as escorting a school visitor to or from the principal's office), the classroom's public address speaker would be requesting the pretty and/or nice-looking white boy or girl. By the time I was in the sixth grade, I was sometimes called by the principal to represent my class because I dressed neatly (I knew this from a progress report sent to my mother, which I translated for her) and because all the "presentable" white girls had moved to the Catholic schools (I later surmised this part). But I was still not one of the popular girls with the boys. I remember one incident where I stepped out into the play-ground in my baggy gym shorts and one Puerto Rican boy said to the other: "What do you think?" The other one answered: "Her face is OK, but look at the toothpick legs." The next best thing to a com-pliment I got was when my favorite male teacher, while handing out the class pictures, commented that with my long neck and delicate features I resembled the movie star Audrey Hepburn. But the Puerto Rican boys had learned to respond to a fuller figure: long necks and a perfect little nose were not what they looked for in a girl. That is when I decided I was a "brain." I did not settle into the role easily. I was nearly devastated by what the chicken pox episode had done to my self-image. But I looked into the mirror less often after I was told that I would always have scars on my face, and I hid behind my long black hair and my books.

After the problems at the public school got to the point where even nonconfrontational little me got beaten up several times, my parents enrolled me at St. Joseph's High School. I was then a minority of one among the Italian and Irish kids. But I found several good friends there—other girls who took their studies seriously. We did our homework together and talked about the Jackies. The Jackies were two popular girls, one blonde and the other red-haired, who had women's bodies. Their curves showed even in the blue jumper uniforms with straps that we all wore. The blonde Jackie would often let one of the straps fall off her shoulder, and although she, like all of us, wore a white blouse underneath, all the boys stared at her arm. My friends and I talked about this and practiced letting our straps fall off our shoulders. But it wasn't the same without breasts or hips.

My final two and a half years of high school were spent in Augusta, Georgia, where my parents moved our family in search of a more peaceful environment. There we became part of a little community of our army-connected relatives and friends. School was yet another matter. I was enrolled in a huge school of nearly two thousand students that had just that year been forced to integrate. There were two black girls and there was me. I did extremely well academically. As to my social life, it was, for the most part, uneventful—yet it is in my memory blighted by one incident. In my junior year, I became wildly infatuated with a pretty white boy. I'll call him Ted. Oh, he was pretty: yellow hair that fell over his forehead, a smile to die for—and he was a great dancer. I watched him at Teen Town, the youth center at the base where all the military brats gathered on Saturday nights. My father had retired from the navy, and we had all our base privileges—one other reason we had moved to Augusta. Ted looked like an angel to me. I worked on him for a year before he asked me out. This meant maneuvering to be within the periphery of his vision at every possible occasion. I took the long way to my classes in school just to pass by his locker, I went to football games, which I detested, and I danced (I too was a good dancer) in front of him at Teen Town—this took some fancy footwork, since it involved subtly moving my partner toward the right spot on the dance floor. When Ted finally approached me, "A Million to One" was playing on the jukebox, and when he took me into his arms, the odds suddenly turned in my favor. He asked me to go to a school dance the following Saturday. I said yes, breathlessly. I said yes, but there were obstacles to surmount at home. My father did not allow me to date casually. I was allowed to go to major events like a prom or a concert with a boy who had been properly screened. There was such a boy in my life, a neighbor who wanted to be a Baptist missionary and was practicing his anthropological skills on my family. If I was desperate to go somewhere and needed a date, I'd resort to Gary. This is the type of religious nut that Gary was: when the school bus did not show up one day, he put his hands over his face and prayed to Christ to get us a way to get to school. Within ten minutes a mother in a station wagon, on her way to town, stopped to ask why we weren't in school. Gary informed her that the Lord had sent her just in time to find us a way to get there in time for roll call. He assumed that I was impressed. Gary was even good-looking in a bland sort of way, but he kissed me with his lips tightly pressed together. I think Gary probably ended up marrying a native woman from wherever he may have gone to preach the Gospel according to Paul. She probably believes that all white men pray to God for transportation and kiss with their mouths closed. But it was Ted's mouth, his whole beautiful self, that concerned me in those days. I knew my father would say no to our date, but I planned to run away from home if necessary. I told my mother how important this date was. I cajoled and pleaded with her from Sunday to Wednesday. She listened to my arguments and must have heard the note of desperation in my voice. She said very gently to me: "You better be ready for disappointment." I did not ask what she meant. I did not want her fears for me to taint my happiness. I asked her to tell my father about my date. Thursday at breakfast my father looked at me across the table with his eyebrows together. My mother looked at him with her mouth set in a straight line. I looked down at my bowl of cereal. Nobody said anything. Friday I tried on every dress in my closet. Ted would be picking me up at six on Saturday: dinner and then the sock hop at school. Friday night I was in my room doing my nails or something else in preparation for Saturday (I know I groomed myself nonstop all week) when the telephone rang. I ran to get it. It was Ted. His voice sounded funny when he said my name, so funny that I felt compelled to ask: "Is something wrong?" Ted blurted it all out without a preamble. His father had asked who he was going out with. Ted had told him my name. "Ortiz? That's Spanish, isn't it?" the father had asked. Ted had told him yes, then shown him my picture in the yearbook. Ted's father had shaken his head. No. Ted would not be taking me out. Ted's father had known Puerto Ricans in the army. He had lived in New York City while studying architecture and had seen how the spics lived. Like rats. Ted repeated his father's words to me as if I should understand *his* predicament when I heard why he was breaking our date. I don't remember what I said before hanging up. I do recall the darkness of my room that sleepless night and the heaviness of my blanket in which I wrapped myself like a shroud. And I remember my parents' respect for my pain and their gentleness toward me that weekend. My mother did not say "I warned you," and I was grateful for her understanding silence.

In college, I suddenly became an "exotic" woman to the men who had survived the popularity wars in high school, who were now practicing to be worldly: they had to act liberal in their politics, in their lifestyles, and in the women they went out with. I dated heavily for a while, then married young. I had discovered that I needed stability more than social life. I had brains for sure and some talent in writing. These facts were a constant in my life. My skin color, my size, and my appearance were variables—things that were judged according to my current self-image, the aesthetic values of the times, the places I was in, and the people I met. My studies, later my writing, the respect of people who saw me as an individual person they cared about, these were the criteria for my sense of self-worth that I would concentrate on in my adult life.

The Chameleon

I caught a chameleon
in my backyard,
and to amuse myself
moved him from a green leaf
to a tree's brown bark,
then to my yellow porch
where he froze as himself
his eyes on me as if waiting
for me to change.

But I stayed the same.

I stayed the same,
and kept him behind a screen
until he had shown me his rainbow,
until he had given me
every color he possessed.

Then I opened the door,
but he wouldn't move.
He just kept his eyes on me
as if waiting for me to change.

The Myth of the Latin Woman: I Just Met a Girl Named María

On a bus trip to London from Oxford University where I was earning some graduate credits one summer, a young man, obviously fresh from a pub, spotted me and as if struck by inspiration went down on his knees in the aisle. With both hands over his heart he broke into an Irish tenor's rendition of "María" from *West Side Story*. My politely amused fellow passengers gave his lovely voice the round of gentle applause it deserved. Though I was not quite as amused, I managed my version of an English smile: no show of teeth, no extreme contortions of the facial muscles—I was at this time of my life practicing reserve and cool. Oh, that British control, how I coveted it. But María had followed me to London, reminding me of a prime fact of my life: you can leave the Island, master the English language, and travel as far as you can, but if you are a Latina, especially one like me who so obviously belongs to Rita Moreno's gene pool, the Island travels with you.

This is sometimes a very good thing—it may win you that extra minute of someone's attention. But with some people, the same things can make *you* an island—not so much a tropical paradise as an Alcatraz, a place nobody wants to visit. As a Puerto Rican girl growing up in the United States and wanting like most children to "belong," I resented the stereotype that my Hispanic appearance called forth from many people I met.

Our family lived in a large urban center in New Jersey during the sixties, where life was designed as a microcosm of my parents' casas on the island. We spoke in Spanish, we ate Puerto Rican food bought at the bodega, and we practiced strict Catholicism complete with Saturday confession and Sunday mass at a church where our parents were accommodated into a one-hour Spanish mass slot, performed by a Chinese priest trained as a missionary for Latin America.

As a girl I was kept under strict surveillance, since virtue and modesty were, by cultural equation, the same as family honor. As a teenager I was instructed on how to behave as a proper señorita. But it was a conflicting message girls got, since the Puerto Rican mothers also encouraged their daughters to look and act like women and to dress in clothes our Anglo friends and their mothers found too "mature" for our age. It was, and is, cultural, yet I often felt humiliated when I appeared at an American friend's party wearing a dress more suitable to a semiformal than to a playroom birthday celebration. At Puerto Rican festivities, neither the music nor the colors we wore could be too loud. I still experience a vague sense of letdown when I'm invited to a "party" and it turns out to be a marathon conversation in hushed tones rather than a fiesta with salsa, laughter, and dancing—the kind of celebration I remember from my childhood.

I remember Career Day in our high school, when teachers told us to come dressed as if for a job interview. It quickly became obvious that to the barrio girls, "dressing up" sometimes meant wearing ornate jewelry and clothing that would be more appropriate (by mainstream standards) for the company Christmas party than as daily office attire. That morning I had agonized in front of my closet, trying to figure out what a "career girl" would wear because, essentially, except for Marlo Thomas on TV, I had no models on which to base my decision. I knew how to dress for school: at the Catholic school I attended we all wore uniforms; I knew how to dress for Sunday mass, and I knew what dresses to wear for parties at my relatives' homes. Though I do not recall the precise details of my Career Day outfit, it must have been a composite of the above choices. But I remember a comment my friend (an Italian-American) made in later years that coalesced my impressions of that day. She said that at the business school she was attending the Puerto Rican girls always stood out for wearing "everything at once." She meant, of course, too much jewelry, too many accessories. On that day at school, we were simply made the negative models by the nuns who were themselves not credible fashion experts to any of us. But it was painfully obvious to me that to the others, in their tailored skirts and silk blouses, we must have seemed "hopeless" and "vulgar." Though I now know that most adolescents feel out of step much of the time, I also know that for the Puerto Rican girls of my generation that sense was intensified. The way our teachers and classmates looked at us that day in school was just a taste of the culture clash that awaited us in the real world, where prospective employers and men on the street would often misinterpret our tight skirts and jingling bracelets as a come-on.

Mixed cultural signals have perpetuated certain stereotypes—for example, that of the Hispanic woman as the "Hot Tamale" or sexual firebrand. It is a one-dimensional view that the media have found easy to promote. In their special vocabulary, advertisers have designated "sizzling" and "smoldering" as the adjectives of choice for describing not only the foods but also the women of Latin America. From conversations in my house I recall hearing about the harassment that Puerto Rican women endured in factories where the "boss men" talked to them as if sexual innuendo was all they understood and, worse, often gave them the choice of submitting to advances or being fired.

It is custom, however, not chromosomes, that leads us to choose scarlet over pale pink. As young girls, we were influenced in our decisions about clothes and colors by the women—older sisters and mothers who had grown up on a tropical island where the natural environment was a riot of primary colors, where showing your skin was one way to keep cool as well as to look sexy. Most important of all, on the island, women perhaps felt freer to dress and move more provocatively, since, in most cases, they were protected by the traditions, mores, and laws of a Spanish/Catholic system of morality and machismo whose main rule was: *You may look at my sister, but if you touch her I will kill you.* The extended family and church structure could provide a young woman with a circle of safety in her small pueblo on the island; if a man "wronged" a girl, everyone would close in to save her family honor.

This is what I have gleaned from my discussions as an adult with older Puerto Rican women. They have told me about dressing in their best party clothes on Saturday nights and going to the town's plaza to promenade with their girlfriends in front of the boys they liked. The males were thus given an opportunity to admire the women and to express their admiration in the form of *piropos*: erotically charged street poems they composed on the spot. I have been subjected to a few piropos while visiting the Island, and they can be outrageous, although custom dictates that they must never cross into obscenity. This ritual, as I understand it, also entails a show of studied indifference on the woman's part; if she is "decent," she must not acknowledge the man's impassioned words. So I do understand how things can be lost in translation. When a Puerto Rican girl dressed in her idea of what is attractive meets a man from the mainstream culture who has been trained to react to certain types of clothing as a sexual signal, a clash is likely to take place. The line I first heard based on this aspect of the myth happened when the boy who took me to my first formal dance leaned over to plant a sloppy overeager kiss painfully on my mouth, and when I didn't respond with sufficient passion said in a resentful tone: "I thought you Latin girls were supposed to mature early"—my first instance of being thought of as a fruit or vegetable—I was supposed to *ripen*, not just grow into womanhood like other girls.

It is surprising to some of my professional friends that some people, including those who should know better, still put others "in their place." Though rarer, these incidents are still commonplace in my life. It happened to me most recently during a stay at a very classy metropolitan hotel favored by young professional couples for their weddings. Late one evening after the theater, as I walked toward my room with my new colleague (a woman with whom I was coordinating an arts program), a middle-aged man in a tuxedo, a young girl in satin and lace on his arm, stepped directly into our path. With his champagne glass extended toward me, he exclaimed, "Evita!"

Our way blocked, my companion and I listened as the man half-recited, half-bellowed "Don't Cry for Me, Argentina." When he finished, the young girl said: "How about a round of applause for my daddy?" We complied, hoping this would bring the silly spectacle to a close. I was becoming aware that our little group was attracting the attention of the other guests. "Daddy" must have perceived this too, and he once more barred the way as we tried to walk past him. He began to shout-sing a ditty to the tune of "La Bamba"—except the lyrics were about a girl named María whose exploits all rhymed with her name and gonorrhea. The girl kept saying "Oh, Daddy" and looking at me with pleading eyes. She wanted me to laugh along with the others. My companion and I stood silently waiting for the man to end his offensive song. When he finished, I looked not at him but at his daughter. I advised her calmly never to ask her father what he had done in the army. Then I walked between them and to my room. My friend complimented me on my cool handling of the situation. I confessed to her that I really had wanted to push the jerk into the swimming pool. I knew that this same man—probably a corporate executive, well educated, even worldly by most standards— would not have been likely to regale a white woman with a dirty song in public. He would perhaps have checked his impulse by assuming that she could be somebody's wife or mother, or at least *somebody* who might take offense. But to him, I was just an Evita or a María: merely a character in his cartoon-populated universe.

Because of my education and my proficiency with the English language, I have acquired many mechanisms for dealing with the anger I experience. This was not true for my parents, nor is it true for the many Latin women working at menial jobs who must put up with stereotypes about our ethnic group such as: "They make good domestics." This is another facet of the myth of the Latin woman in the United States. Its origin is simple to deduce. Work as domestics, waitressing, and factory jobs are all that's available to women with little English and few skills. The myth of the Hispanic menial has been sustained by the same media phenomenon that made "Mammy" from *Gone with the Wind* America's idea of the black woman for generations; María, the housemaid or counter girl, is now indelibly etched into the national psyche. The big and the little screens have presented us with the picture of the funny Hispanic maid, mispronouncing words and cooking up a spicy storm in a shiny California kitchen.

This media-engendered image of the Latina in the United States has been documented by feminist Hispanic scholars, who claim that such portrayals are partially responsible for the denial of opportunities for upward mobility among Latinas in the professions. I have a Chicana friend working on a Ph.D. in philosophy at a major university. She says her doctor still shakes his head in puzzled amazement at all the "big words" she uses. Since I do not wear my diplomas around my neck for all to see, I too have on occasion been sent to that "kitchen," where some think I obviously belong.

One such incident that has stayed with me, though I recognize it as a minor offense, happened on the day of my first public poetry reading. It took place in Miami in a boat-restaurant where we were having lunch before the event. I was nervous and excited as I walked in with my notebook in my hand. An older woman motioned me to her table. Thinking (foolish me) that she wanted me to autograph a copy of my brand new slender volume of verse, I went over. She ordered a cup of coffee from me, assuming that I was the waitress. Easy enough to mistake my poems for menus, I suppose. I know that it wasn't an intentional act of cruelty, yet of all the good things that happened that day, I remember that scene most clearly, because it reminded me of what I had to overcome before anyone would take me seriously. In retrospect I understand that my anger gave my reading fire, that I have almost always taken doubts in my abilities as a challenge—and that the result is, most times, a feeling of satisfaction at having won a convert when I see the cold, appraising eyes warm to my words, the body language change, the smile that indicates that I have opened some avenue for communication. That day I read to that woman and her lowered eyes told me that she was embarrassed at her little faux pas, and when I willed her to look up at me, it was my victory, and she graciously allowed me to punish her with my full attention. We shook hands at the end of the reading, and I never saw her again. She has probably forgotten the whole thing but maybe not.

Yet I am one of the lucky ones. My parents made it possible for me to acquire a stronger footing in the mainstream culture by giving me the chance at an education. And books and art have saved me from the harsher forms of ethnic and racial prejudice that many of my Hispanic *compañeras* have had to endure. I travel a lot around the United States, reading from my books of poetry and my novel, and the reception I most often receive is one of positive interest by people who want to know more about my culture. There are, however, thousands of Latinas without the privilege of an education or the entrée into society that I have. For them life is a struggle against the misconceptions perpetuated by the myth of the Latina as whore, domestic or criminal. We cannot change this by legislating the way people look at us. The transformation, as I see it, has to occur at a much more individual level. My personal goal in my public life is to try to replace the old pervasive stereotypes and myths about Latinas with a much more interesting set of realities. Every time I give a reading, I hope the stories I tell, the dreams and fears I examine in my work, can achieve some universal truth which will get my audience past the particulars of my skin color, my accent, or my clothes.

I once wrote a poem in which I called us Latinas "God's brown daughters." This poem is really a prayer of sorts, offered upward, but also, through the human-to-human channel of art, outward. It is a prayer for communication, and for respect. In it, Latin women pray "in Spanish to an Anglo God / with a Jewish heritage," and they are "fervently hoping / that if not omnipotent, / at least He be bilingual."

Saint Rose of Lima

> Never let my hands be to any one
> an occasion for temptation.
>
> —Isabel de Flores

She was the joke of the angels—a girl
crazy enough for God

that she despised her own beauty; who grew bitter herbs
to mix with her food,

who pinned a garland of roses to her forehead;
and who, in a fury of desire

concocted a potion of Indian pepper and bark
and rubbed it on her face, neck, and breasts,

disfiguring herself.
Then, locked away in a dark cell,

where no reflection was possible,
she begged for death to join her with her Master

whom she called *Divine Bridegroom, Thorn
in My Heart, Eternal Spouse.*

She would see His vague outline, feel His cool touch
on her fevered brow,

but as relief came, her vision would begin to fade,
and once again she would dip the iron bar into the coals,

and pass it gently like a magician's wand over her skin—
to feel the passion that flames for a moment,

in all dying things.

Counting

An oriental ink drawing:
a shadowy range of mountains,
and a gray lake rising. Pneumonia
is the name of the country on the lighted screen,
the chest of my two-year-old daughter.
                                        At home
in her pink eggshell room,
I dig blindly in drawers for clothes,
and for something familiar and comforting
to take her at the hospital.
My fingers are caught in a string of beads,
the rosary my mother
has had the priest bless for my child's birthday:
"Teach her to count on Christ," instructed
the accompanying card.
                        A disbeliever
in the power of objects, I allow this penitent's jewelry,
the chain of linked sets of beads,
to slip through my fingers, joining my hands
into the steeple of an unsteady temple.
The part of my brain
I never listen to anymore begins
a litany of prayers in my mother's voice. I hear
myself joining in, counting down deep enough
to where I can believe
that beads of amber glass can be magical.

Unspoken

When I hug you tight at bedtime
you wince in pain for the tender
swelling of new breasts.
Nothing is said, both of us aware
of the covenant of silence
we must maintain through the rending
apart that is adolescence.
        But it won't always
be confusion and hurting, the body
will find itself through this pain;
remember Michelangelo, who believed
that in marble, form already exists,
the artist's hands simply pulling it out
into the world.
        I want to tell you about men:
the pleasure of a lover's hands on skin
you think may rip at elbows and knees
stretching over a frame like clothes
you've almost outgrown; of the moment
when a woman first feels
a baby's mouth at her breast, opening her
like the hand of God in Genesis, the moment
when all that led to this seems right.
        Instead I say, *sweet dreams,*
for the secrets hidden under the blanket
like a forbidden book

I'm not supposed to know you've read.

Who Will Not Be Vanquished?

—For Tanya

1.
I named you for a snow-princess
in a Russian novel,
a woman of noble bearing
who would not be vanquished
by war nor passion: not Lara,
the other one—the quiet aristocrat
who inspired no poems from the man
but for whom he walked the frozen miles.

2.
Gold earrings flashing
through your black hair, you pirouette
so that your wide skirt blooms
around the long stems of your legs
for me to admire your wild beauty.
You are transformed
into one of the gypsy ancestors
we have never discussed.

3.
On the fall day of your birth,
in a city not far enough north
of the equator for my fantasy,
I held onto *Doctor Zhivago*
so hard, that when the first pain came,
I broke the spine. While the hot wires
announcing your arrival shot through me,

I imagined a sleigh pulled
by strong white horses, gliding
over a landscape of powdery snow.
In the distance: an ice palace.

4.
Today you want to go somewhere exotic:
an island in the Caribbean
inhabited only by beautiful young people;
a place where a girl might pick
from anyone's garden, a red hibiscus
for her hair, and wear a dress so light
that any breeze might make it dance;
where a dark-haired man
wearing a flowered shirt
leans against the bright blue wall
of a café, holding a guitar,
waiting for inspiration.

5.
Mourning suits us Spanish women.
Tragedy turns us into Antigone—maybe
we are bred for the part.

6.
Your best friend, also fifteen,
leaped from her father's speeding car
during an argument. After the call,
I saw how your eyes darkened
as you listened to my careful words;
I saw the women of our family in black,
gathering in a circle around you.

7.
On the ride to the hospital,
you sit up straight, averting your gaze.
I place my hand on your trembling shoulder,
and assure you that it's OK to cry.
But, gently, you disengage yourself
from my intrusive touch.
Without looking back, you walk away from me,
and into the antiseptic castle where she waits
like a captive maiden in her costume of gauze.

8.
She waits there, regal in her pain, eager
to recount her wingless flight, to show you
her wounds, and to tell you
about the betrayals of parents.

Hostages to Fortune

In three days, I would have to send her down
into the ground, which treats no differently
excrement, snakeskin, daughter, worm—

if a dream of flight took her too far to return,
as if blown off course by a storm. Trembling,
at 3:00 A.M., I am standing by her bed
and her body is too still. Yet,
I hesitate to place my hand on her chest,

to feel it rise and fall with her breath,
as I did in her childhood, waking like this,
as I used to often, nearly sleepwalking,
even when her sleep was full and deep
after a day's hard play.

Now she wears a bone-tight skin of nerves.

How would I survive this: touching a cool,
alabaster statue in the morning; or the vision
of tan skin melting like wax from her bones,
of her long, slim body—a ruin for study—
female human, sixteen years of age, maybe older.

She was clearly in good health, they will say,
strong—no evidence of having given
any hostages to fortune.

To a Daughter I Cannot Console

Last night I called my mother long distance
to talk about your sadness. After years
of separation, our tone is forgiving,
our word choices careful; the turmoil
of our kinship now in subscript to the text
of our separate sorrows.
                              I told her of the tears
that keep pouring out of that infinite well
that a broken heart is at sixteen. She spoke
the inevitable "it will pass," asking me
to remember the boy I had cried over for days.
I could not for several minutes
recall that face.

And her consolation was true.
It has to do with time—what we both know now
as enemy to the flesh; also
as the healer of wounds. But for you,
there are no words that will help. Time to you
is a slow clock measuring the rise of beauty,
the deepening of feeling.
                              It is too late
for the tokens of motherhood; the distraction
of a new toy, a bedtime story, a hug; too soon
to convince you that the storm surging within
will abate—like all acts of God.
                              And the heart,
like a well-constructed little boat, will resume
its course toward hope.

Anniversary

Lying in bed late, you will sometimes read to me
about a past war that obsesses you;
about young men, like our brothers once,
who each year become more like our sons
because they died the year we met,
or the year we got married
or the year our child was born.
                                    You read to me
about how they dragged their feet through a green maze
where they fell, again and again, victims
to an enemy wily enough to be the critter hero
of some nightmare folktale, with his booby traps
in the shape of human children, and his cities
under the earth; and how, even when they survived,
these boys left something behind
in the thick brush or muddy swamp where no one
can get it back—caught like a baseball cap
on a low-hanging tree branch.

                    And I think about you and me,
nineteen, angry, and in love, in that same year
when America broke out in violence
like a late-blooming adolescent, deep in a turmoil
it could neither understand nor control;
how we marched in the rough parade
decorated with the insignias of our rebellion:
peace symbols and scenes of Eden
embroidered on our torn and faded jeans,
necks heavy with beads we did not count on

for patience, singing *Revolution*—
a song we misconstrued for years.
                              Death was a slogan
to shout about with raised fists or hang on banners.

But here we are,
listening more closely than ever to the old songs,
sung for new reasons by new voices. We are survivors
of an undeclared war someone might decide to remake
like a popular tune. Sometimes, in the dark, alarmed
by too deep a silence, I will lay my hand on your chest,
for the familiar, steady beat to which I have attuned
my breathing for so many years.

5:00 A.M.: Writing as Ritual

An act of will that changed my life from that of a frustrated artist, waiting to have a room of my own and an independent income before getting down to business, to that of a working writer: I decided to get up two hours before my usual time, to set my alarm for 5:00 A.M.

When people ask me how I started writing, I find myself describing the urgent need that I felt to work with language as a search; I did not know for a long time what I was looking for. Although I married at nineteen, had a child at twenty-one—all the while going through college and graduate school *and* working part-time—it was not enough. There was something missing in my life that I came close to only when I turned to my writing, when I took a break from my thesis research to write a poem or an idea for a story on the flip side of an index card. It wasn't until I traced this feeling to its source that I discovered both the cause and the answer to my frustration: I needed to write. I showed my first efforts to a woman, a "literary" colleague, who encouraged me to mail them out. One poem was accepted for publication, and I was hooked. This bit of success is really the point where my problem began.

Once I finished graduate school, I had no reason to stay at the library that extra hour to write poems. It was 1978. My daughter was five years old and in school during the day while I traveled the county, teaching freshman composition on three different campuses. Afternoons I spent taking her to her ballet, tap, and every other socializing lesson her little heart desired. I composed my lectures on Florida's I-95, and that was all the thinking time I had. Does this sound like the typical superwoman's lament? To me it meant being in a constant state of mild anxiety which I could not really discuss with others. What was I to say to them? I need an hour to start a poem. Will someone please stop the world from spinning so fast?

I did not have the privilege of attending a writers' workshop as a beginning writer. I came to writing instinctively, as a dowser finds an underground well. I did not know that I would eventually make a career out of writing books and giving readings of my work. The only models I knew were the unattainable ones: the first famous poet I met was Richard Eberhart, so exalted and venerable that he might as well have been the Pope. All I knew at that time was that at twenty-six years of age I felt spiritually deprived, although I had all the things my women friends found sufficiently fulfilling in a "woman's life" plus more; I was also teaching, which is the only vocation I always knew I had. But I had found poetry, or it had found me, and it was demanding its place in my life.

After trying to stay up late at night for a couple of weeks and discovering that there was not enough of me left after a full day of giving to others, I relented and did this odious thing: I set my alarm for five. The first day I shut it off because I could: I had placed it within arm's reach. The second day I set two clocks, one on my night table, as usual, and one out in the hallway. I had to jump out of bed and run to silence it before my family was awakened and the effort nullified. This is when my morning writing ritual that I follow to this day began. I get up at five and put on a pot of coffee. Then I sit in my rocking chair and read what I did the previous day until the coffee is ready. I take fifteen minutes to drink two cups of coffee while my computer warms up—not that it needs to—I just like to see it glowing in the room where I sit in semidarkness, its screen prompting "ready": ready whenever you are. When I'm ready, I write.

Since that first morning in 1978 when I rose in the dark to find myself in a room of my own—with two hours belonging only to me ahead of me, two prime hours when my mind was still filtering my dreams—I have not made or accepted too many excuses for not writing. This apparently ordinary choice, to get up early and to work every day, forced me to come to terms with the discipline of art. I wrote my poems in this manner for nearly ten years before my first book was published. When I decided to give my storytelling impulse full rein and write a novel, I divided my two hours: the first hour for poetry, the second for fiction; two pages minimum per day. Well or badly, I wrote two pages a day for three and one-half years. This is how my novel, *The Line of the Sun*, was finished. If I had waited to have the time, I would still be waiting to write my novel.

My life has changed considerably since those early days when I was trying to be everything to everyone. My daughter is eighteen and in college, not a ballerina, Rockette, or horsewoman but a disciplined student and a self-assured young person. Thus I do not regret the endless hours of sitting in tiny chairs at the Rock-Ette Academy of Dance or of breathing the saturated air at the stables as I waited for her. She got out of her activities something like what I got out of getting up in the dark to work: the feeling that you are in control, on the saddle, on your toes. Empowerment is what the emerging artist needs to win for herself. And the initial sense of urgency to create can easily be dissipated because it entails making the one choice many people, especially women, in our society with its emphasis on the "acceptable" priorities, feel selfish about making: taking the time to create, stealing it from yourself if it's the only way.

The Medium's Burden

In the morning kitchens of my friends,
I must gather the dreams they spill
like bread crumbs on the table.
Over coffee and easy talk, I see
their lives swirling in my cup.

Virginia's restless night
yields an old woman in rags,
Medusa eyes turning everything
to stone: her husband frozen on their bed
against the wall, the baby
in his crib becomes a statue of Cupid,
even the dog, a bark stuck in his throat,
is petrified at the door.

Cristina is buried alive, tucked into the grave
by loved ones. She claims a sense of peace
in her coffin, where she sleeps deeply
under the thick, warm, comforter of earth.

They must ask me what it means, and I
must say. Either way, speech or silence,
means I have stayed beyond my welcome.

In my own recurring dream,
I am the woman in the painting
whose mouth is sealed in a smile
beneath the pentimento, whose eyes
break through the canvas to watch

the anonymous crowds drift by,
throwing me their casual glances
like alms in a cup. I know their hearts,
and I am tormented forever
by knowing.